Jim, all thing ... possible
to the one ...
Pat

Pat Colli

Expectant Faith

AND THE POWER OF GOD

the columba press

First published in 1998 by
the columba press
55a Spruce Avenue, Stillorgan Industrial Park
Blackrock, Co Dublin

Cover by Bill Bolger
Cover photograph is a detail from
The Rimini School: *The Crucifixion and Noli me tangere,*
used by permission of the National Gallery of Ireland
Origination by The Columba Press
Printed in Ireland by Colour Books Ltd, Dublin
ISBN 1 85607 183 9

Contents

Foreword

The many forms of natural and supernatural faith are fascinating. Charismatic faith is particularly intriguing. It is characterised by intense trust in God which can lead to remarkable results. For example, I remember an English woman with multiple sclerosis, who was paralysed from the neck downward. A Polish student and a friend prayed over her for ten minutes. Afterwards she made a complete recovery, and resumed her teaching career. I know woman in Northern Ireland who prayed for a crippled boy from the travelling community who was suffering from a congenital bone disease. He immediately began to improve and finally his callipers were removed. Nowadays he is attending school and is able to play football. A few years ago a woman in a Dublin parish encouraged fellow parishioners to join her in praying publicly for the parish priest who was nearing death from lung cancer. From that time on he made a rapid and complete recovery. I know a Protestant couple who were led by the Spirit to buy a property for use as a retreat centre. They trusted in divine providence and asked God to supply the necessary cash. Almost miraculously they received enough donations to pay their monthly bills. I have noticed that in all these incidents, and many others beside, the power of God was manifested as a result of trusting faith of an unhesitating, expectant kind.

Although numerous books have been written about different aspects of faith, apart from fleeting references, exegetes and theologians have largely neglected its charismatic form. As far as I'm aware no one has written a systematic study of this gift. A couple of years ago I was visiting Seton Hall, a Catholic University in New Jersey. A computer buff helped me to do a sophisticated electronic search of the 300,000 books and journals in the library.

We looked for anything that might deal with the charism of faith. We didn't find as much as an article! Truly, it is a neglected gift. Subsequently I did some research on the topic and wrote a post-graduate thesis entitled 'Charismatic faith in 1 Cor 12:9 and elsewhere in the New Testament.'

Some time ago, I was thinking about the fact that in 1998, Catholics will prepare for the Millennium Jubilee by focusing on the role of the Holy Spirit. Pope John Paul II has stated that: 'The primary task of the preparation for the Jubilee includes a renewed appreciation of the presence and activity of the Spirit, who acts within the Church both in the Sacraments, especially in Confirmation, *and in the variety of charisms*, roles and ministries which he inspires for the good of the Church.'[1] In the light of those words I decided that I would try to make a modest contribution to those preparations by writing a book on what seems to be the most anonymous of the charisms.

Converting a thesis into a book isn't easy. I imagine its a bit like trying to turn a stage-play into a movie script. From the beginning I had a fundamental choice to make, whether to write in a popular anecdotal style, or in a more systematic, scholarly way. In the end I decided to compromise. I wrote new chapters, rewrote and rearranged others, while retaining relevant scholarly points. I hope that they will be helpful to those who have an academic interest in the charism of faith. Wherever possible, I pared down the text by removing pedantic details and non-essential footnotes. I also tried to relate different aspects of the charism of faith to everyday life and sought to illustrate what I meant by practical examples.

This study is motivated by a number of desires. It is my hope that it will introduce interested readers to the place of the charism of faith in a continuum that ranges from doctrinal to trusting faith. I also hope that it will throw light on Jesus' many references to the importance of belief. It is my growing conviction that he may have exercised this kind of faith himself, and that when he commended those who had faith and admonished those who did not, he had in mind the unhesitating trust that is characteristic of charismatic faith. I hope too that the book will enable Pentecostals and Charismatics, in particular, to have a deeper appreciation of the pivotal role of charismatic faith within the range of the gifts listed in 1 Cor 12:8-10. Furthermore, I hope that this study will renew understanding of the strategic importance of charismatic faith in such things as the anointing of the sick and the new evangelisation called for by Pope John Paul II.

Different chapters will have reason to refer to the prayer of petition and command, together with deeds of power such as healing, exorcism and miracle working. They prompt the question. Does God intervene in nature by over-riding its physical laws? Currently a number of scientists, philosophers and theologians are attempting to deal with the complex issues that a considered answer would involve.[2] Suffice it to say that I don't personally believe that God interferes *ad extra*, i.e. from outside, with the laws of nature. Whereas, the Lord does seem to break the laws of nature as they are currently understood, there is good reason to believe that in the not too distant future, those laws will be revised within the context of a more all-embracing conception of reality. As St Augustine reminded us in *The City of God* (XXI, 8), 'A miracle is contrary not to nature but to what is known of nature.' The Rev John Polkinthorne a scientist and theologian working in Oxford has stated that miracles 'can only find theological acceptance if they are perceived as part of a wider unity of divine action and purpose, which goes beyond the experience of everyday but which forms with it a coherent whole. The pursuit of such a unified understanding is the main task of theology in the face of the unexpected which we call the miraculous.'[3] The unified understanding Polkinthorne refers to will probably include the inter-connectedness of everything, i.e. of physical laws, transpersonal psychology and the realm of the Spirit. It will indicate how, besides being transcendent, God is immanent in reality through the deeds of power performed by human beings. They fulfil potentials already latent in creation as it is elevated to a higher realm and therefore to different 'laws.'

I want to take this opportunity of thanking the members of the Vincentian community in St John's University, New York City, for their generous hospitality during a six-month sabbatical from September 1995 to March 1996. They afforded me the time and facilities to research the subject matter of this book while offering emotional support, encouragement and scholarly help. This volume is dedicated to all of them with gratitude and warm appreciation. I also want to thank two colleagues, Frs Jim McCormack C.M. and James Murphy C.M. of All Hallows College, Dublin, for reading my original manuscript and making such perceptive and helpful suggestions. I'm indebted to Angela Mc Anespie for proofing the manuscript. My grateful acknowledgements are also due Bernard Tracey O.P., editor of *Doctrine and Life*, for permission to include a modified version of an article entitled, 'Models of Evangelisation' in chapter eleven.[4]

A couple of points about the use of terminology in the book. By and large the phrases charism of faith, charismatic faith, unhesitating faith, and expectant faith are synonymous in meaning. I should also explain that, where possible, I have tried to avoid sexist language, especially when referring to God. As a result many references to the Lord, such as Godself, are awkward and abstract.[5] That is inevitable when personal pronouns such as 'him' and 'himself' are dropped. Finally, I'm painfully aware that in spite of my best efforts, and the help of others, this is a provisional introduction to the subject of charismatic faith. Its shortcomings are entirely my responsibility. It will have been worthwhile, however, if at some time in the future, others more competent than I, challenge, correct and develop the understanding of expectant faith which is presented here.

CHAPTER ONE

The Charism of Expectant Faith in Context

Many years ago I came across the writings of Joachim of Fiore (1132-1202 A.D.). Besides being the abbot of the monastery in Calabria in Southern Italy, he was a mystic and a theologian. One Pentecost Sunday, while chanting the Psalms, he had a visionary experience to do with the mystery of the Trinity. Afterwards he made the fascinating suggestion that there are three stages in salvation history. The first was the age of the Father (the Old Testament). The second stage, in which Joachim himself lived, was the age of the Son (the New Testament and many generations afterwards). The third stage was the coming age of the Spirit which would be characterised by deep spirituality, and a quasi-direct contact with the presence and guidance of God. It would be a time when the feminine aspects of religion would come into their own. Speaking about the characteristics of the three stages he said: 'In the first infants are taught, in the second adolescents are formed, in the third friends are inebriated.'[1] Ever since reading that prophecy, I have wondered, are we the fortunate ones who are living in the promised age of the Spirit? There are good reasons for thinking that we are.

A remarkable religious event has been occurring in the twentieth century. The Pentecostal and Charismatic movements, which have been referred to as the 'third force' in Christianity, have augmented the more traditional forces of Catholicism-Orthodoxy and Protestantism. As Peter Hocken has suggested, this ever expanding river has been the result of the confluence of five main tributaries.[2]

The first, fresh stream, originated in 1906, at Apostolic Faith Mission, Azusa Street, Los Angeles, when an inter-racial group of poor people, who were led by a black pastor called William

Joseph Seymour, experienced a powerful outpouring of the Holy Spirit and his gifts. These included speaking in tongues and prophecy. The mainline churches to which these Christians belonged couldn't accept the new phenomenon, so they split off and formed their own churches, such as the Church of God, and the International Pentecostal Holiness Church. Over the years these denominations have developed their own distinctive forms of theology spirituality and worship.

The second stream arose in the late 1950's and the early '60's when members of the mainline Protestant Churches were influenced by Pentecostals and experienced the outpouring of the Spirit and his gifts. Instead of leaving their denominations, as the Pentecostals before them had done, many of these Episcopals, Baptists, Methodists, etc., formed the Protestant Charismatic Movement. They did so with a view to renewing their own churches from within.

The third stream was formed when people who had been Baptised in the Spirit – mainly in the Protestant Churches – left their respective denominations because they felt they were moribund and beyond renewal. They formed what are known as 'house churches.' Whereas denominational Charismatics have focused on the charisms in 1 Cor 12:8-10, these non-denominational groupings have also emphasised ministry gifts, mentioned in Eph 4:11, such as those of apostle, prophet, evangelist, pastor and teacher.[3] In recent years these non-denominational groupings have spread throughout the world. For example it is estimated that, whereas there are 6 million denominational Charismatics in the US there are 14 million of the independent kind.[4]

The fourth stream appeared with the surprising emergence of Messianic Judaism in the late 1960's. Jewish people who have accepted Jesus as the promised Messiah are not inclined to call themselves either Christian or Charismatic, because of the negative connotations these terms might have for Jewish people. However, as Peter Hocken, has pointed out, Messianic Judaism is predominately Charismatic and aims to integrate Jewish forms of worship with a faith filled confession of Jesus as Messiah.[5]

The fifth stream welled up in the mid 1960's when Catholics

(1)

(Acts 3:1-10) Solemnity of Saints Peter and Paul on June 29th).
Maybe sometimes we are like that beggar,

Settling for too little, begging for pennies

so much more that God wants to give us.

Maybe sometimes we get lost during life counting the pennies,

God has plans walk and jump and praise him.

Maybe even the whole Church settles for too little like the beggar, while God has plans for much more,

that the Church should walk and jump and praise God.

That beggar was unchanging and unquestioning.

That beggar met the love of God and was changed forever.

(God entered his heart)

first began to experience the in-filling of the Holy Spirit and the charismatic gifts. Because this book is being written from a Catholic perspective, it is worth recounting the way in which this happened. The growth of the modern Catholic Charismatic Movement was anticipated, in a prophetic way, when the Second Vatican Council discussed the subject of lay ministry and the charisms of the Holy Spirit. There were two schools of thought. The traditionalists, led by Cardinal Rufini, argued in Augustinian terms that the charisms were granted to the early church in order to get it firmly established. When Christianity took root in the Greco-Roman world the charisms mentioned in 1 Cor 12:8-10 were no longer needed, and died out rather quickly. Ever since, these particular charisms have been extremely rare and only granted to exceptionally holy people in order to confirm their sanctity and to manifest the divine presence and power.[6] St Augustine had written: 'These miracles are not allowed to continue into our time, lest the soul should always require things that can be seen, and by becoming accustomed to them mankind should grow cold towards the very thing whose novelty had made men glow with fire.'[7] In the following year, i.e. 426 A.D., Augustine modified his earlier view in a book entitled *Retractions.* He wrote: 'What I said should not be taken as understanding that no miracles are believed to happen today in the name of Christ.'[8] He then went on to explain that at the very time of writing, many such miracles had been reported in his diocese.

The progressives, led by Cardinal Suenens argued that charisms, ordinary and extraordinary alike, were granted to the faithful for the edification of the church. He said: 'The remarks made about the charisms of the Christian people are so few that one could get the impression that charisms are nothing more than a peripheral and unessential phenomenon in the life of the Church. Now the vital importance of these charisms for building up the Mystical Body must be presented with greater clarity and consequently at greater length. What is to be completely avoided is the appearance that the hierarchical structure of the Church seems to be an administrative apparatus with no intimate connection with the charismatic gifts of the Holy Spirit which are spread throughout the life of the Church ... Does not each one of us know lay people, both men and women, in his own diocese who are truly called by God? These people have received various different charisms from the Spirit, for catechesis, evangelisation, apostolic action of various types, social work, and charitable activity ... Without these charisms, the ministry of the Church would be impoverished and sterile.'[9]

In the event the second point of view, which was supported by scripture scholars attending the Council as invited experts, prevailed. The main teaching of the bishops appeared in part two of paragraph twelve of the *Dogmatic Constitution on the Church*. This teaching was adverted to again in paragraph three of the *Constitution on the Laity*. During his pontificate, Paul VI, often spoke about the gifts of the Spirit.[10] His talks elaborated on the meaning and implications of the conciliar teachings. In recent years, Pope John Paul II has reiterated this teaching in paragraph twenty four of the post synodal document entitled, *The Vocation and Mission of the Laity*. The *Catechism of the Catholic Church* also mentions the charisms in pars. 799-801 and 2003.

The teaching of these documents can be summarised in the following eight points:

1. Grace comes to us not only through sacraments and clerical ministry, but also through the charisms of the Spirit, including the list of charisms mentioned in 1 Cor 12:8- 12, which includes the charism of faith.
2. The Holy Spirit distributes what are variously referred to as simple/ordinary/widely diffused/humble gifts; and outstanding/exceptional/great/extraordinary gifts, among lay people.
3. These gifts are given to build up the church in holiness and to develop people.
4. The charisms are a wonderful means of apostolic vitality.
5. These gifts are to be received with gratitude and consolation.
6. Lay people have a right to exercise their charisms and ministries. This right comes from their baptism and not from the clergy.
7. Lay people have a duty to use their charisms for the good of the church and the world.

8. Bishops and clergy should test the charisms to see that they are genuine and used for the common good. However, they should be careful not to quench the Spirit by an arbitrary use of authority.

A New Pentecost

The Catholic Charismatic movement began in 1967. By then it was already apparent that the church was undergoing considerable difficulties in the post-Vatican II era. Theologian, Charles Davis probably got to the heart of the matter when he wrote in *America* on January 29th 1966: 'Much speaking in different places on themes of renewal has brought me into contact with many people seeking to revivify their faith. I have found a sense of emptiness, but together with it a deep yearning for God. There is an emptiness at the core of people's lives, an emptiness waiting to be filled. They are troubled about their faith; they find it slipping. I am not speaking of those who are worried about recent changes. These people are not. But they are looking for something more; they are looking for something to fill the void in their lives, and what they hear does not do that. The more perceptive know they are looking for God ... Who will speak to them quite simply of God as of a person he intimately knows, and make the reality and presence of God come alive for them once more?'

During this time of religious unrest, some students, from Duquesne University, met for a weekend of prayer and fasting. According to Kevin and Dorothy Ranaghan their state of mind was similar to the one described by Davis: 'There was something lacking in their individual Christian lives. They couldn't quite put their finger on it, but somehow there was an emptiness, a lack of dynamism, a sapping of strength in their lives of prayer and action. It was as if their lives as Christians were too much their own creation, as if they were moving forward under their own power and of their own will. It seemed to them that the Christian life wasn't meant to be a purely human achievement.'[11]

Each of the people who attended the retreat read *The Cross and the Switchblade,* the first four chapters of the Acts of the Apostles and asked for a new outpouring of the Holy Spirit.

Afterwards they claimed to have experienced a release of the Spirit and his charismatic gifts. The Ranaghans said that the blessing they received wasn't a separate grace from the one received in baptism and confirmation: 'It seemed, rather, a kind of adult re-affirmation and renewal of these sacraments, an opening of ourselves to all their sacramental graces.'[12] Soon, an ever increasing number of American Catholics began to have similar experiences. Prayer groups quickly sprang up all over the country, in universities, parishes, monasteries and convents. Within a relatively short period of time the movement spread to all the five continents. For example, the Charismatic Movement came to Northern and Southern Ireland in the early seventies.[13] Writing in *L'Osservatore Romano* on Jan 2nd 1975, Prof Marie-Joseph Le Guillou, went so far as to say that with the 'liberation' of the charisms 'we are certainly at the dawn of a new era in the history of the Church.'

By 1990 the Vatican estimated that there were about 11.8 million active Catholic Charismatics all over the world and estimated that there would be 23.1 million in the year 2000. It is also said that in 1990 that there were an estimated 60.3 million post-charismatics, i.e. people who were at one time or another affiliated to the movement, and projected that there would be 86.8 million in the year 2000. That would mean that taken together that there were 72.1 million Charismatics and post-charismatics in 1990 and that there could be as many as 109.9 million at the beginning of the new millennium. This is a striking and significant statistic. In the space of 35 years or so, the Catholic Charismatic Movement will have influenced 9.3% of the church's membership. As such it is probably the fastest growing movement within the contemporary world-wide Catholic community.

The Growth of Pentecostalism and the Charismatic Movements

Whereas traditional forms of Catholicism and Protestantism have experienced decline in the 20th century, especially in Western countries, the combined Pentecostal and Charismatic movements have been growing rapidly. For example, in 1992 the World Council of Churches estimated that in the previous three years in Rio de Janeiro, 700 new Pentecostal churches had been opened. In spite of an increasing population, only one new

Catholic parish was established in the city during the same period. Between 1985 and 1990 the Anglican and Catholic churches in Britain lost about 10% of their members, whereas during the same period the membership of the Pentecostal and so called charismatic 'House Churches' had increased by about 30%. It is estimated that currently there may be as many as 400 million Pentecostals worldwide.[14] As one church statistician has commented: 'The sheer magnitude and diversity of the numbers involved beggar the imagination ... The Pentecostals and Charismatics, and third-wavers who make up this Renewal today number 21% of organised global Christianity ... One quarter of the world's full-time Christian workers are Pentecostals or Charismatics.[15]

Why does the third force in Christianity seem to be more successful than the other two more traditional forms? To answer this question Harvey Cox refers to the researches of a French scholar Daniele Hervieu-Leger. She maintains that the centre of gravity of modern religion is shifting from objective religious authority to subjective religious experience. Sociological research has confirmed that this is so.[16] John C. Haughey has pointed out that those who focus on experience do not live according to theological principles but according to a felt knowledge, an inner unction that the Spirit provides. Affective prayer is normally the context in which this experience of God occurs. Pentecostals and Charismatics are inner directed people, but the inner to which they attend, is 'The Beyond within.'[17] This trend is particularly evident in Pentecostal and Charismatic groups. Cox says that the religious authorities in the Catholic and Protestant Churches are uneasy about two aspects of this approach. Firstly, because of a strong emphasis on lay ministry 'the traditional clergy plays a less privileged role.' Secondly he observes: 'The other feature of "experiential" spirituality that religious professionals resent is that today's seeker is often looking for some very practical results. The postmodern pilgrims are more attuned to a faith that helps them find the way through life here and now. There is something quite pragmatic about their religious search. Truths are not accepted because someone says they are true, no matter what that leader's religious authority may be, but because people find that they connect, they "click" with their own everyday existence.'[18]

It could be added that those in authority in the traditional churches are afraid that this experiential approach to religion could lead to subjectivism and end in factionalism and even schism. While this has been the case in the Pentecostal Movement, by and large it has not been true of the Charismatic movements within the Protestant and Catholic churches. The Pentecostal-Charismatic experience has two main characteristics, Baptism in the Spirit, and the exercise of the charisms mentioned in 1 Cor 12:8-10. We will briefly look at both points.

Baptism in the Holy Spirit

While it is true that we receive the Holy Spirit in a *sacramental way* in baptism and confirmation, we need to appropriate those graces in an *experiential way* later in life as a result of baptism in the Spirit.[19] It is a religious experience, that inaugurates a decisively new awareness of God's loving presence and power at work in one's life. It is the power in the words of Eph 3:18-19 to grasp: 'Together with all the saints, how wide and long and high and deep is the love of Christ, and to know this love that surpasses knowledge – that you may be filled to the measure of all the fullness of God.' This spiritual awakening is often associated with the reception of one or more of the charismatic gifts mentioned by St Paul in 1 Cor 12:8-10.The Irish bishops have described baptism in the Spirit as 'a conversion gift through which one receives a new and significant commitment to the Lordship of Jesus and openness to the power and gifts of the Holy Spirit.'[20]

Whereas Pentecostals see it as a second blessing, distinct from salvation, Catholics and others see Baptism in the Spirit as an experiential release of the graces already received in the sacraments of baptism and confirmation.[21] Authors George Montague and Killian McDonnell have said that their reading of the relevant biblical and Patristic texts has led them to the conviction that the baptism in the Holy Spirit is an *integral* aspect of Christian initiation.[22] They show that in the first eight centuries of Christian history it was assumed that when adults received the sacraments of initiation, they would not only be baptised in the Spirit, they would also receive the gifts of the Holy Spirit, those mentioned in Is 11:2 and those in 1 Cor 12:8-10 as well. For example, In a treatise on baptism Tertullian (160-225 A.D.) said to those who had received the sacrament: 'you should open your hands and pray with your brothers and sisters, ask the Father, ask the Lord that to the grace of baptism a very special gift may be added, the distribution of the *charismata*.'[23] As a result Montague and McDonnell make the challenging assertion, that the baptism in the Holy Spirit is *normative* for *all* Christians.[24]

The Charisms in 1 Cor 12:8-10

As we have mentioned already, it is only when people have experienced baptism in the Spirit, that they can expect, to exercise one or more of the charismatic gifts mentioned in 1 Cor 12:8-10. They are grace given abilities, which equip men and women for acts of service that contribute to the animation and up-building of the church. They can have a number of good effects.

Firstly, the charisms can play an important, if not a central role in lay-ministry. Lay people are no longer supposed to be the inferior, passive recipients of clerical ministry. Rather, they are called and gifted to be active partners with the clergy in bringing the good news into every aspect of secular life. Current church documents, e.g. par. 31 of *The Lay Members of Christ's Faithful People,* use the phrase lay 'apostolate' in preference to lay 'ministry,' because, although clerical and lay roles are complementary, they are distinct.

Secondly, the charisms have an important role to play in the New Evangelisation called for by the present Pope. Many Christians believe that we should go beyond presence evangelisation to engage in what is sometimes known as power evangelisation. The former witnesses to the good news mainly by means of loving relationships and liberating action for justice. The latter believes that the charisms of power, which are rooted in the charism of faith, also have an important role to play. As manifestations of the presence and power of the Lord (1 Cor 12:7) they can be used to revive the faith of the lapsed and to evangelise unbelievers. We will return to this subject in the final chapter.

Thirdly, the charisms have an important ecumenical role to play. Happily the Spirit and his gifts have been poured out in all denominations. Through their common exercise, Christians are being drawn closer to Jesus and therefore closer to one another. In an article entitled, 'Ecumenical Origins of the Charismatic Renewal,' Peter Hocken shows clearly that renewal in the Spirit and reconciliation have been virtually synonymous in the Charismatic Renewal.[25] Charisms, as Christians in Northern Ireland and elsewhere recognise, have a unique ability to build bridges of unity.

Fourthly, the charisms have an important mystical dimension. Mysticism, according to its historical and psychological definitions, is the direct intuition or experience of God; and a mystic is a person who has, to a greater or less degree, such a direct experience – one whose religion and life are centred, not merely on an accepted belief or practice, but on that which he or she regards as first-hand personal knowledge.[26] In an essay entitled, *The Spirituality of the Future,* Karl Rahner wrote, 'The Christian of the future will be a mystic or he or she will not exist at all, if by mysticism we mean....a genuine experience of God emerging at the very heart of our existence.'[27] I believe that there is a mystical aspect to the charisms. In his authoritative book, *Christian Mysticism,* Harvey Egan has shown how many of the gifts, including the charism of faith, could be classified as secondary mystical phenomena, which are characteristic of the illuminative stage of spiritual growth.[28] For example, praying in tongues can be understood as an imageless, conceptless form of contemplative prayer similar in nature and effects to the Jesus Prayer. The charism of faith could be seen as a direct rapport with the dynamic of God's loving purpose and power.

The charism of faith, which is the focus of this study, has been defined as: 'a supernatural surge of confidence from the Spirit of God which arises when a person receives a trans-rational certainty and assurance that God is about to act through a word or action ... It is both an irresistible knowledge of God's intervention at a certain point and the authority to effect his intervention through the power of the Holy Spirit.'[29] Although a great deal of writing has been done on particular charisms, such as tongues, prophecy, healing and discernment of spirits, the charism of faith has been almost totally neglected. For example in his book *Showing the Spirit: A Theological Exposition of 1 Corinthians 12-14,* [30] D. A. Carson includes a nineteen page long bibliography of relevant commentaries, books and dissertations on the charisms and related topics. In spite of its length, it fails to make a single explicit reference to the charism of faith. Although Michael O' Carroll's *Veni Creator Spiritus: Theological Encyclopaedia of the Holy Spirit* [31] is large and long, there are only three and a half lines devoted to the charism of faith. It is much the same with Avery Dulles's scholarly masterwork, *The Assurance of Things Hoped For: A Theology of Christian Faith.* It too, only devotes only a few lines to the charism of faith. While there has been a good deal of writing about healing of a charismatic and sacramental kind, it usually overlooks the central role of the charism of faith in both. For example, Kelsey's book *Christianity and Healing* and McManus's *Healing and the Sacraments* say very little about this particular charism.

The Aim of the Book

From a theological point of view this book intends to show how the charism of faith is different from other related forms of trust. It will highlight the nature, characteristics, and importance of this charism. This will be done by examining and evaluating relevant texts in the bible, the writings of the Church Fathers, the theology of Thomas Aquinas and the witness of some modern Charismatics. It will suggest that this particularly intense, unhesitating form of trust is a key that unlocks the meaning of scripture texts to do with God's willingness to answer prayer and the believer's ability to perform deeds of power such as healings, miracles and exorcisms. It will also seek to establish that more often than not, when Jesus spoke about firm faith, commended those who had it, and admonished those who hadn't, he probably had the charism of faith in mind. It will also examine contemporary arguments for and against the contention that Jesus himself exercised the charism of faith.

It is my belief that the extent to which we fail to appreciate the charism of faith, is the extent to which we will tend to rationalise many scriptural promises in a reductionist way. But when the charism of faith is properly understood, it has practical implications for intercessory prayer, effective evangelisation, and powerful ministry.

Methodology

It seems to me that many contemporary scripture scholars and theologians have espoused, to a greater or lesser extent, a post-Enlightenment perspective. As Pope John Paul has written: 'The rationalism of the Enlightenment was supposed to put to one side the true God – in particular, the God of the Redeemer.'[32] In many instances the God of revelation seems to have been replaced with a more secularised one. For example, the Kantian God is unknowable and beyond the world, so much so, that for all intent and purposes we have to get on without the Deity. The Hegelian God, on the other hand, is so immanent in the dialectics of history and thought as to be almost synonymous with enlightened humanism.

It would appear that many modern theologians and students of the New Testament, e.g. Bultmann, seem to interpret the scriptures in terms of reductionist assumptions of this kind. As a result they fail to do justice to the mind and meaning of the inspired authors, especially when it comes to the role of charismatic faith in deeds of power such as healings and miracles. As John Meier has written: 'The miracles were signs and partial realisations of what was about to come fully in the kingdom. Commentators who accept all this nevertheless often seek to explain the exorcisms and cures in terms of psychological suggestion, while dismissing the more intractable nature miracles. Such a judgment is based not on historical exegesis but on a philosophical *a priori* about what God can or cannot do in the world, an *a priori* rarely if ever defended with rigorous logic. Instead, appeal is made to "modern man," who looks suspiciously like 18th century Enlightenment man.'[33] This study will try to avoid such *a priori* assumptions by focusing on what the various authors were intending to say and which their written words conveyed.

This study will involve a good deal of textual analysis. It will rely on the findings of reputable scripture scholars in particular. The aim, throughout, will be to uncover the meanings intended by the respective authors in order to see what light they, may or may not, throw upon the nature and characteristics of the charism of faith. By employing methods such as form criticism, which tries to trace the origin and history of particular passages by analysing their structural forms, and redaction criticism, which investigates the editorial work done by biblical authors on earlier material, contemporary scripture scholars try to go beyond the Christ of faith in order to discover the actual words and works of the Jesus of history. While the following chapters take some account of that distinction, they will be informed by the belief that in the last analysis it is not of central importance, as far as this book is concerned. After all, while Christians believe that the word of God in the gospels is ultimately dependent upon the Jesus of history, it bears *inspired* witness to the Christ of faith. What is important is 'the sense which the human author directly intended and which the written words conveyed.'[34] This study will also take account of what modern scholars say about the authorship of New Testament letters, such as those ascribed to Paul. Ultimately, this is not an issue of crucial importance either, because all the letters, regardless of their authorship, are the inspired word of God.

There will be a constant effort to get behind the objective content of texts in order to sense the subjective faith experiences, of a religious kind, that they express. In recent years, a number of theologians have acknowledged the importance of this dimension of scriptural, patristic and theological texts.[35] There has been a good deal of writing about the nature of religious experience. It is a notoriously difficult term to define. In this book it, will refer, not to the second order activity of talk or thought *about* God, i.e. belief, but rather to an immediate, conscious, awareness *of* God, one which is mediated in one way or another by the twin bibles of creation and the scriptures, i.e. faith. However, as Dorr and Dulles have pointed out,[36] when such faith experiences are articulated in a conceptual way, they inevitably become interpretations, because all theological reflection is influenced by cultural and religious paradigms which are historically conditioned, and by the intellectual and emotional strengths, prejudices, and preoccupations of the one who theologises.

Many people, like myself, claim to have had charismatic experiences, including experience of the charism of faith. From an interpretative point of view, this is an important point, because first hand experience of the charism, can enable the graced person, whether he or she is a scholar or not, to interpret what is recounted in the scriptures, and elsewhere, in a more sympathetic way. For example, in the early church many of the fathers had direct or indirect charismatic experience, and were consequently self-assured in their interpretation of 1 Cor 12:8-10. But once the charisms died out, the later fathers were not nearly so authoritative in their exegesis of that passage. For example, St John Chrysostom (347-407 A.D.) said with great insight and honesty: 'This whole passage 1 Cor 12:8-12, is very obscure; *but the obscurity is produced by our ignorance of the facts referred to,* (my italics) and by their cessation, being such as then used to occur, but now no longer take place.'[37] This interpretative principle, will have to be kept in mind when looking at what the fathers of the Church and St Thomas had to say about the charisms, specifically the charism of faith. There is no compelling evidence that either Thomas or the people he knew, exercised charisms such as tongues, interpretation of tongues, healing or miracle working.

Conversely, an accurate understanding of the scriptures, can be used not only as a means of detecting inaccurate understandings of the charism of faith in patristics and theology, it can also be used to correct the inadequate interpretations and beliefs of some Pentecostals and Charismatics. A number of exegetes warn that Charismatics can interpret what Paul says about the gifts, including the gift of faith, in an unjustifiable way. For example, Jerome Murphy O' Connor has written: 'The list of gifts in 1 Cor 12:1-11, is not exhaustive and precise definitions are impossible. Many of the meanings assumed by charismatic groups are arbitrary.'[38] Raymond Brown says much the same: 'No person reared in the 20th century has the wordview of a person reared in the 1st century, and therefore it is impossible today to know or duplicate what Paul describes, no matter how genuine the self-assurance of the charismatic.'[39] The truth is most likely to emerge when scholarship and experience are mutually interdependent, each one throwing a critical light on the other. Scholarship without experience is dead, while experience without scholarship is blind.

Conclusion

At the beginning of this chapter I wondered whether we are living in the age of the Spirit. In 1975 Pope Paul VI indicated, in *Evangelii Nuntiandi* that the age of the Spirit might well have arrived when he wrote in par 75: 'We live in the Church at a privileged moment of the Spirit. Everywhere people are trying to know Him better, as the Scripture reveals Him. They are happy to place themselves under His inspiration. They are gathering about Him; they want to let themselves be led by Him.' Around that same time I heard German theologian, Heribert Muhlen, say that as a result of changes like those mentioned by the Pope, the focus of theology was shifting from Christology to Pneumatology. I believe that events since then have been proving him to be correct.

CHAPTER TWO

Forms of Faith

Faith plays a fundamental role in life and religion. Erik Erikson's developmental psychology suggests that the first task that a newborn child has to tackle is whether to trust or mistrust its primary carers, usually its mother and to a lesser extent its father. The ability to trust is evoked by the baby's perception of the reliability of the carers, their willingness to meet its physical and emotional needs. If they are consistently available and responsive, the child's sense of trust will be wholehearted. But the extent to which the carers are undependable is the extent to which the child's ability to trust will be compromised. This will be particularly noticeable in early adulthood between the ages of twenty and forty, approximately, when the primary developmental task is whether to love or not, i.e. a choice between forming intimate relationships with significant others and remaining isolated. If an adult is not very trusting, he or she will find it more difficult to form loving relationships of a committed type. This will be evident in a reluctance to share personal secrets and deeper feelings, especially of a vulnerable kind. Because grace builds on nature, it's not surprising that there is an affinity between the dynamics of natural and supernatural trust. As Erickson has written: 'Trust born of care is, in fact, the touchstone of the actuality of a given religion.'[1]

As far as religious faith is concerned, theologians point out that it can be looked at from two separate but interrelated points of view. Firstly, faith can be looked at as a *noun* in so far as it refers to the objective truths that are believed. It is commonly referred to in Latin terminology as the *fides quae*. Secondly, faith can be looked at as a *verb* in so far as it refers to the subjective act of believing. In Latin it is referred to as the *fides qua*. So although it can have many contents, scholars, ancient and modern, have suggested that there are only two basic forms of faith, doctrinal and trusting. For example in the 4th century, St Cyril of Jerusalem said in one of his catechetical sermons that the word 'faith' had two meanings. 'First of all, it is concerned with doctrine and it denotes the assent of the soul to some truth.' Then he added, 'The word "faith" has a second meaning: it is a particular gift and grace of Christ.'[2] He went on to explain that this gift of grace is a form of trust which reaches its most intense form in mountain moving faith.

The same distinction is made in Orthodox theology. For example, in the fourteenth century the monks Callistus and Ignatius of Xanthopoulos wrote, 'Faith is of two kinds.' They went on to say that the first was the faith into which people were baptised. People who had the second kind: 'Being enriched by the Divine light of grace, they put all their hope in the Lord to such measure that, in accordance with the word of our Lord (Mk 11:23), when they pray they do not think in their hearts about their petitions to God, but with faith both ask and readily receive what is needful.' The two authors then proceed to describe the mystical awareness of the unitive kind that is characteristic of people who have exercised such firm faith. 'These blessed men,' they say, 'acquired such firmness of faith through pure works, because they had steadfastly renounced all knowledge, speculation and hesitation and freed themselves of all cares and totally absorbed in the Divine rapture of faith, hope and love of God.'[3]

In the early 1950's Jewish scholar, Martin Buber, explored this distinction in depth in his *Two Types of Faith: A Study of the Interpretation of Judaism and Christianity.*[4] It maintained that trust in God was the predominant Jewish form of faith in the Old Testament and the gospels, whereas, assent to revealed truth was, by and large, the principal Christian form of faith in one or two of the New Testament epistles and church history. In the foreword of his book he says: 'There are many contents of faith, but we only know faith itself in two basic forms. Both can be understood from the simple data of our life: the one from the fact that I trust someone, without being able to give sufficient reasons for my trust in him; the other from the fact that, likewise without being able to give a sufficient reason, I acknowledge a thing to be true.'[5] Later he adds: 'The acceptance of the truth acknowledged by me can lead to contact with the one whom it proclaims. But in the former instance it is the existent contact which is primary, in the latter the acceptance is accomplished.'[6]

The *Catechism of the Catholic Church* endorses the distinction between the two types of faith. It says: 'faith is first of all a personal adherence of man to God' (i.e. trusting faith). Then it adds: 'At the same time and inseparably, it is free assent to the whole truth God has revealed' (i.e. faith as assent).[7] In par 397 it says that as a result of original sin 'All subsequent sin would be disobedience toward God and *lack of trust* in his goodness' and in Par 154 goes on to make it clear that a person adheres to God principally by means of trust.

By way of generalisation, it would probably be true to say that within Christianity, Protestant evangelicalism with its roots in Lutheranism and Calvinism, tends to emphasise the centrality of faith as trust. On the other hand, Catholicism, especially in the Counter Reformation era, has tended to emphasise the centrality of faith as assent to the doctrines taught by the church. For example, at the first Vatican Council faith was described as: 'a supernatural virtue by which with the inspiration and help of God's grace, we believe that what he has revealed is true – not because its intrinsic truth is seen with the natural light of reason - but because of the authority of the God who reveals it.'[8]

Trust in the Old Testament

The rest of this chapter, as indeed the rest of this book will concentrate on faith as trust in God. We can begin by saying that biblical faith is not a static belief in God's existence. It is taken for granted. As Ps 53:1 explains: 'Only the fool says in his heart there is no God.' In the scriptures, faith, is seen in dynamic terms as firm conviction, firstly, about the attributes of Yahweh, e.g. God's loving kindness and compassion, and secondly, about God's willingness to act in a saving and liberating way in accordance with the divine nature and promises. This distinction is illustrated by Goethe's Faust. When he was translating the first verse of John's Gospel we are told that he began by writing: 'In the beginning was the Word!,' then he tried, 'In the beginning was the Thought!,' then he went on to, 'In the beginning was the

Power!,' Finally he wrote: 'The Spirit is helping me! I see now what I need and write assured: In the beginning was the Deed.'[9] God, is not so much the God who exists as the One who acts.

A) Hebrew words for trust

In the Old Testament the chosen people enjoyed an on-going religious experience of the One who revealed the Godself to them by means of the wonderful events of salvation history, e.g. the escape from captivity in Egypt and the making of the covenant at Sinai. In Deut 7:9 we read: 'Know therefore that the Lord your God is God; he is the faithful God, keeping his covenant of love to a thousand generations of those who love him and keep his commands.' In Hebrew the verb for being 'faithful' is *amen*. It literally means 'to be firm; to endure; to be true; to stand fast.'[10] The noun which describes God's faithfulness is *emunah*. It was derived from the root *'mn*: "to be stable."' Unger and White maintain that in the Old Testament *emunah* is synonymous with the notion of righteousness, loving kindness and justice.[11] In Hos 2:19-20 God is said to manifest these attributes: 'I will betroth you to me forever; I will betroth you in righteousness and justice, in love and compassion. I will betroth you in faithfulness, and you will acknowledge the Lord.' A second Hebrew word *betach*, was also used to describe God's faithfulness. It literally means 'security, or trust.'[12] It was the Israelites awareness of God's abiding faithfulness and reliability that evoked in them the graced ability to trust in God.

In Hebrew the word for the act of trusting is also *amen*, which can mean 'to have belief; to believe.' In other words the overlapping meanings of the word *amen*, suggest that we can trust in God because God is trustworthy. Three verses encapsulate the biblical attitude: 'Trust in the Lord with all your heart, and lean not on your own understanding,' Prov 3:5, and again: 'Commit your way to the Lord; trust in him and he will act' Ps 37:5 and finally, Jer 17:7 says: 'Blessed are those who trust in the Lord, whose trust is in the Lord.'

B) Trusting in God's word

Because the Jews trusted in God, they trusted that the Lord would act in accordance with the divine promises. Yahweh's word was as sure as it was unique. In Western culture words describe pre-existing reality. In the bible, however, God's word is constitutive of reality. It contains the power to effect what it says. As George Montague points out, 'When the Hebrew speaks a word, he is not taking in the outside world and shaping it within himself. Rather he is thrusting something creative and powerful outward from himself into the external world and actually changing that world.'[13] For example, in Gen 1:3 'God said, "Let there be light," and there was light.' As Is 55:10-11 says: 'As the rain and the snow come down from heaven, and do not return to it without watering the earth and making it bud and flourish, so that it yields seed for the sower and bread for the eater, so is my word that goes out from my mouth: It will not return to me empty, but will accomplish what I desire and achieve the purpose for which I sent it.' In Jer 49:13 the Lord swears by his own divine authority and faithfulness to act, and in Ezech 36:36 God says: 'I Yahweh have spoken (i.e. promised such and such...) and shall do it.' As Heb 11 points out, the heroes and heroines of faith in the Old Testament were blessed, precisely because they relied, with unwavering trust, in the sure and certain promises of God. It adds in verse six that: 'Without faith it is impossible to please God.'

C) Abraham as model

Abraham is the model of this kind of faith. He and his aged wife Sarah were without children. Then God manifested the divine presence to Abraham. Because he was sure of Yahweh, he was equally sure of the promise made by God. Despite the fact the he and his wife were senior citizens, they believed the angel who told them they would have a son who would be the father of a great nation, which would be as numberless as the stars in the heavens and the grains of sand on the sea shore. Because he trusted in the God of the word, Abraham trusted in the word of God. He believed, in spite of the evidence of reason and the senses, that it would be fulfilled. As Heb 11:11 states: 'By faith he received the power of procreation, even though he was too old - and Sarah herself was barren – because he considered him faithful who had promised.'

In due course Isaac was born. His name meant laughter, because the people had laughed when Abraham and Sarah maintained that they would bear the son of promise. When Isaac was born, it was they and God who had the last laugh. Later on Yahweh tested Abraham. He asked him to sacrifice his beloved son, the one on whom the fulfillment of the promises depended. Because he placed unconditional trust in God, Abraham was willing to kill his boy. At the last moment the Lord stayed his hand by the message of an angel and spared Isaac. Speaking about Abraham, St Paul was later to comment admiringly in Rom 4:20-21: 'He did not waver through unbelief regarding the promise of God, but was strengthened in his faith ... being fully convinced that God was able to do what he had promised.'

Faith in the New Testament

Not surprisingly there is a great deal of continuity between the Old and New Testament conceptions of faith. In the *New Revised Standard Version* of Heb 11:1 this form of trust is described in these words: 'Now faith is the assurance of things hoped for, the conviction of things not seen.' When the Greek words *elenchos* and *hypostasis* are respectively translated as 'assurance' and 'conviction,' the emphasis is focused on subjective dispositions. But a number of reputable scripture scholars argue that the two words can be translated in a more objective way as 'reality' and 'demonstration.' Faith in that case is the reality of the goods hoped for, the proof of things one cannot see. This point, concerning the subjective and objective dimensions of faith in St Paul, will be mentioned again. At this stage suffice it to say that there is no real conflict between the two. Subjective conviction is based on objective authority.

A) The language of Faith in the New Testament

Meantime it can be noted that three interrelated Greek words are involved in the New Testament writings, *pisteuo* a verb which means, 'I believe;' *pistos* an adjective meaning, 'faithful,' or 'believing, and *pistis*, a noun which means 'faith.' In both classical and biblical Greek, *pistis* refers to 'the act of giving one's trust.'[14] These Greek words were used by the Septuagint translators in place of the Hebrew *emunah*.

The Greek noun *pistis* can be translated as 'faithfulness, fidelity, trustworthiness, reliability, pledge, oath, or assurance', and therefore includes the notion that God is a trusted person, firm and reliable.

Depending on the context, the verb *pisteuo* 'to believe,' can have a number of shades of meaning. Firstly, it can mean 'to obey.' For example, Rom 1:8 talks about: 'the obedience of faith.' Secondly, it can mean: 'to trust', e.g. in Rom 10:11, Paul says: 'No one who trusts in him will be put to shame.' Thirdly, to believe can also mean 'to hope,', e.g. speaking of Abraham, Rom 4:18 says: 'He believed, hoping against hope.' Scripture scholars[15] draw attention to the fact that in the New Testament two important phrases are used, namely, *pisteuein eis*: 'to believe in' and *pisteuein hoti*: 'to believe that.' They are like two sides of the same coin of doctrinal and trusting faith, distinct but inseparable. For example because of their faith in Christ, Christians believe that Jesus is Lord, and that his promises are true. As Dermot Lane observes: 'The act of faith in the New Testament is a highly personal and existential act addressed to God. It also includes a cognitive component, not in terms of propositions but in terms of recognising and perceiving the truth as well as appropriating that truth.'[16]

The adjective *pistos*, can mean either 'faithful' or 'trusting.' In this sense God and Christ can be relied on. For example, speaking about the ability to resist temptation, St Paul writes: 'God is faithful, and will not let you be tempted beyond your strength, but with the temptation will also provide the way of escape' 1 Cor 10:13. The notion of God's faithfulness is also reiterated in, 2 Cor 1:18, and 2 Tim 2:13.

B) Three types of trusting faith

A number of years ago Steve Clark suggested in his book *Growing in Faith* that there were three forms of faith discernible in the New Testament, especially in the gospels, namely, believing, trusting and expectant. He says that believing faith could be referred to as doctrinal or propositional faith. Trusting faith involves confidence in the goodness, benevolence and providence of God. Expectant faith goes further in that it is convinced that God will act in specific circumstances of need in accordance with the divine promises. In Mk 5:24-34, the woman with the chronic bleeding problem exercises this kind of expectant faith. Instead of saying with trusting faith 'If I touch his garments I may get well if it is God's will,' she says with expectant faith, 'If I touch his garments I will get well.' I have come to the conclusion that although Clark's distinction is perceptive it is slightly confusing. Consistent with a point made above, I would suggest that there are two basic forms of faith, doctrinal and trusting, and that there are three kinds of trusting faith. The first is a form of trust in divine providence. The second and third, are forms of trust in God's promise to respond to petitionary prayers in a saving and liberating way. Needless to say, promises to answer prayer are an expression of divine providence.

Firstly, trust in the providence of God. The Lord has a plan for our lives and makes provision so that we can carry it out. No matter what happens, even negative experiences are embraced by God's love. Evil will not have the last word, it belongs to God, and it is a saving word of victory. As Rom 8:28 says: 'All things work together for good for those who love God, who are called according to his purpose.'

Secondly, there is wishful trust of a hesitating kind. It desires that God would act in accordance with his attributes and promises, but it does so in a doubt-filled way which lacks inner conviction. Jm 1:7-8 adverts to this kind of faith when he says that doubters are like 'a wave on the sea driven and tossed by the wind.'

Thirdly, there is expectant trust of an inspired, un-hesitating kind. It is sure of God's willingness to act in accordance with the divine attributes and promises. It does so with firm conviction. Jesus refers to this kind of faith when he says in Mk 11:24: 'Whatever you ask for in prayer, believe that you have received it, it will be yours.'

These distinctions are important because they will be adverted to, again and again, throughout the book. At this point suffice it to say that the charism of faith, as we shall try to show, is a form of unhesitating trust which is repeatedly referred to in the gospels and epistles.

C) Faith in the Pauline epistles

When St Paul uses the word *pistis*, the Greek word for faith, it refers primarily to the object of the act of believing, i.e. God and divine faithfulness, and only in a secondary and subordinate way to the faith of the believer. As a result, scripture scholars[17] point out that when Paul talks about faith in Jesus Christ, and through him in the Father, he wants to tell us about the Lord, about the fact that God can be trusted completely. This is so because divine faithfulness and trustworthiness are beyond question. As the author of 2 Tim 2:13 testifies: 'If we are faithless, he remains faithful.' Bultmann has this to say about the apostle's conception of faith: 'Paul like the New Testament generally, does not describe the growth of faith in terms of its psychological development ... Paul shows faith to be a historical rather than a psychological possibility. According to Paul, the event of salvation history is actualised for the individual, not in pious experience, but in his baptism Gal 3:27-29.'[18]

A careful reading of the epistles indicates that St Paul refers to at least five interrelated forms of faith; creedal; saving; faith as a fruit of the Spirit; trusting faith and the charism of faith. They are like five different facets of the same precious stone. Before going on to look, in a detailed way, at charismatic faith in 1 Cor 12:9 and other verses in the Pauline writings, it is important to situate that investigation within the wider context of the apostle's thinking about the interconnected forms of faith.

Creedal Faith

On the road to Damascus, Paul had his first and decisive Christian experience. Over the years, not only did that experience deepen, he articulated it in his many letters. Like other first century Christians, he helped to create the creed, i.e. a statement of what is believed. When he talks about the Christian gospel, Paul sometimes refers to it as 'the faith.' In Gal 1:23, he humbly reveals that the early Christians said of him after his conversion: 'He who once persecuted us, is now preaching the faith he once tried to destroy.'

Saving Faith

It is quite clear that saving or justifying faith lies at the heart of Pauline theology, and develops the Old Testament notion of faith. Indeed Joachim Jeremias says that Paul expressed in theological concepts intuitions Jesus had expressed in parables and images.[19] For example it seems to me that the notion of justification by faith in Gal 2:16, expresses what was implicit in Jesus' parable about the prodigal son. He was accepted back into the family home, not because of any personal merit, but because he trustfully accepted that his Father's love was unconditional. Briefly put, saving faith involves at least four interconnected elements.

Firstly, there is an acknowledgment of *need*, and a desire for salvation e.g. the despairing Roman jailer who cried out to Paul and Silas, 'What must I do to be saved?' Acts 16:30.

Secondly, the needy person has to hear the kerygma or core teachings of the Christian *faith*.[20] As Paul wrote, 'How can they believe in him of whom they have not heard? Faith comes from what is heard, and what is heard comes through the word of Christ' Rom 10:14;17.

Thirdly, as Acts 16:31 points out, it is by believing in the Lord Jesus Christ, rather than trusting in their own efforts or merits, that people are *saved*. As Paul declared, 'We have come to believe in Christ Jesus, so that we might be justified by faith in Christ, and not by doing the works of the law' Gal 2:16.

Fourthly, belief leads to *confession*. Paul expressed it this way: 'If you confess with your mouth that Jesus is Lord and believe in your heart that God raised him from the dead, you will be saved. For one believes with the heart and so is justified, and one confesses with the mouth and so is saved' Rom 10:9-10.

Faith as a Fruit of the Spirit

In Gal 5:22 Paul refers to a third kind of faith, when he writes: 'But the fruit of the Spirit is love, joy, peace, patience, kindness, goodness, faith, gentleness, self-control.' In modern bibles the Greek word for faith is variously translated as 'faithfulness,' 'fidelity,' and 'trustfulness.' Unlike the charism of faith which is a special grace, faith as a fruit of the Spirit, is the expression of Christian character, the outcome of the heart's graced union with the Lord. It finds expression in two interconnected effects, firstly, confident trust and dependence on God in all things, and secondly, trustworthiness. For Paul, to believe in Christ is to put one's trust in him. As a result of trust in God, the Lord's trustworthiness and fidelity are reproduced in the believer.[21] This is the essence of faith as a fruit of the Spirit. Paul acknowledges that he bore this fruit: 'I have fought a good fight, I have finished my course, I have kept the faith' 1 Tim 6:9.

Faith as trust in God

The Pauline epistles do not refer to trusting faith very often. But there are a number of passages which express trust in the goodness and providential care of God. For example in Rom 8:35 we read: 'Who shall separate us from the love of Christ? Shall trouble or hardship or persecution or famine or nakedness or danger or sword? As it is written: "For your sake we face death all day long; we are considered as sheep to be slaughtered." No, in all these things we are more than conquerors through him who loved us.' Again in Heb 13:5-6 we read in similar vein: 'Keep your lives free from the love of money and be content with what you have, because God has said, "Never will I leave you; never will I forsake you."' So we say with confidence, 'The Lord is my helper; I will not be afraid. What can man do to me?' Finally in Rom 5:11 Paul says: 'We are filled with joyful trust in God, through our Lord Jesus Christ through whom we have already gained our reconciliation.'

Faith as a Charism

There are at two certain references to the charism of faith in the Pauline epistles. In 1 Cor 12:9 the apostle says: 'to each is given the manifestation of the Spirit for the common good ... to another *faith* by the same Spirit.' In 1 Cor 13:2 he says: 'If I have all faith, so as to move mountains, but do not have love I am nothing.' The next chapter will look at other possible Pauline references to the charism of faith. At this point suffice it to say that they refer to unhesitating trust of an expectant kind in the inspirations and promises of God which often find expression in deeds of power such as healings and miracle working.

D) Faith and inspired knowledge

Paul's understanding of faith is rich and subtle. The interrelationship of faith and inspired knowledge is a key element in his conception of belief. This point is worthy of special attention because it will come up again in relation to the charism of faith. While St Paul was opposed to the false, occult knowledge, of the pagans, he believed in inspired knowledge of an orthodox Christian kind that evokes faith. Through faith in Christ a person is granted a Spirit given understanding, which reaches beyond the limitations of purely rational forms of knowing. As he says in 1 Cor 2:9-16, 'what no eye has seen, nor ear heard, nor the human heart conceived ... God has revealed to us through the Spirit; for the Spirit searches everything, even the depths of God.' No wonder then that in Eph 1:17-18 Paul prayed 'that the God of our Lord Jesus Christ ... may give you a spirit of wisdom and revelation in the knowledge of him, having the eyes of your heart enlightened.'

Arthur Wallis has observed: 'There is no faith without revelation. As at conversion, so throughout the Christian life, impartation of faith, strengthening of faith, increase of faith involve a continuing work of revelation.'[22] Noted Pauline scholar Herman Ridderbos supports this point of view when he makes the significant general observation: 'These concepts *pistis* (i.e. faith) and *gnosis* (inspired knowledge) define each other reciprocally in the Pauline conception of faith.'[23] In saying this, Ridderbos echoes what St Clement of Alexandria (140-216 A.D.) had already stated: 'There is no gnosis (inspired knowledge) without *pistis* (faith), and there is no *pistis* (faith) without *gnosis* (inspired knowledge), just as there is no Father without the Son.'[24] We will return to this point in the next chapter when examining the probable connection between the charisms of wisdom and knowledge in 1 Cor 12:8, and the charism of faith in 1 Cor 12:9.

E) Mary as exemplar of trusting faith

If Abraham is the model of trusting faith in the Old Testament, Mary is undoubtedly the exemplar of trusting faith in the New. When the angel appears to her and announces that she will be the mother of Jesus, she is confused. She asks, how can she, an unmarried virgin, conceive a child? Gabriel declares that it will be made possible through the overshadowing of the Holy Spirit as nothing is impossible to God. Because she enjoys an intimate relationship with God, Mary expresses expectant trust of an unhesitating kind when she replies, 'let it happen to me as you have said' Lk 1:38. Some time later, Mary visits Elizabeth who is also expecting a child. The older woman declares that her younger cousin is blessed, not primarily because she is full of grace, or the mother of the coming messiah, but because 'she ... believed that the promise made her by the Lord would be fulfilled' Lk 1:45.

Conclusion

The opening paragraph asserted that, because nature and grace are interconnected, there is an affinity between natural and supernatural trust. A child's ability to trust its parents is not a matter of choice, rather it is evoked by its awareness of the goodness and reliability of its carers. It is the same in our relationship with God. We cannot choose to trust in the Lord. Trust of whatever kind, is evoked by our graced perception of who God is and what God is like. The only choice we can make is to decide whether to respond to the evocation or not. The decision not to do so can be influenced by such things as rationalism, an unwillingness to surrender control, and unresolved feelings of unworthiness. Faith of a trusting kind, however, including the charism of faith, is rooted in a contemplative awareness of the divine nature and attributes. The extent to which a person has an intimate relationship with the Lord, is the extent to which he or she will be sure of God's willingness to fulfil the divine promises.

CHAPTER THREE

The Charism of Expectant Faith in the Epistles of Paul

Our study of the charism of faith begins with St Paul's first epistle to the Corinthians. There are two reasons for this. Firstly, this letter was probably written in 54 or 55 A.D. From a chronological point of view it predates the synoptic gospels by anything between fifteen to twenty years. Secondly, 1 Cor 12:9 and 1 Cor 13:2 contain the only unambiguous references to the charism of faith in the New Testament. Our examination is conducted within the wider context of Paul's teaching about faith which was mentioned in chapter two. We will begin by looking at the charism of faith within the ambit of Paul's teaching on the charisms in general, i.e. as spirituals, gifts of grace, forms of power, manifestations of God, and services for the up-building of the community. Then we will look at the relationship of the charism of faith to the charisms of wisdom and knowledge on the one hand, and the charisms of healing and miracle working on the other. We will go on to propose a provisional definition of the charism of faith. In the light of that definition, we will evaluate other problematic references in Paul's epistles, one in his second letter to the Corinthians the others in his letter to the Romans. The chapter will end with a brief look at the relationship of the charism of faith to *agape*, i.e. unconditional Christian love.

St Paul on the Charism of Faith

From the time of his conversion, onwards, faith played a central role in the ministry and writings of St Paul. As he testified in Gal 2:20, 'The life that I am now living, subject to the limitations of human nature, I am living in faith, faith in the Son of God who loved me and gave himself for me.' Faith can be looked at from two points of view, subjective and objective. There is the believer's *experience* of faith, and the *object* of his or her act of faith. As was noted in chapter 2 when St Paul uses the word 'faith', it refers principally to the object of the act of believing, i.e. God and God's faithfulness, and only in a secondary and subordinate way to the faith of the believer. As a result, scripture scholars[1] point out that when Paul talks about faith in Jesus, or the Father, he wants to tell us about the Lord, about how God can be trusted completely. This is so because divine faithfulness and trustworthiness are beyond question (cf. 2 Tim 2:13)

A) Characteristics of the charism of faith

We have already looked at the forms of faith in the Pauline letters. Now our attention can begin to focus on the charism of faith which St Paul refers to when he says: 'To one is given through the Spirit the utterance of wisdom, and to another the utterance of knowledge according to the same spirit, *to another faith* by the same Spirit' 1 Cor 12:8-9. In 1 Cor 12 he uses five different words to describe the gifts of the Spirit in general and therefore of the charism of faith in particular.

The Charism of Faith as a Spiritual

St Paul introduces the subject of the spiritual gifts early in the epistle: 'you are not lacking in any spiritual gift as you wait for the revealing of our Lord Jesus Christ' 1 Cor 1:7. He returns to the same topic in 1 Cor 12:1. What he says in the Greek is: 'now concerning the *pneumatika*.' In its Pauline usage the word could be taken to refer to 'spiritual people.' If Paul had this meaning in mind, verse one would be translated: 'Now concerning spiritual people.' However it is more likely that it should be translated, 'now concerning the spirituals', i.e. the charisms. In the light of later Catholic theology, it can be argued that implicit in this verse is the belief that grace builds on nature. For example, in the case of the charism of faith, the Holy Spirit enhances and transforms the natural capacity to trust. There could also be an eschatological dimension to the word. In a spirit of hope the spirituals, especially the charism of faith, span the chasm between the 'is' and the 'not yet' of the Christian life. Understood in this way the 'spirituals' are a foretaste of the way the Spirit will transform some things in the near future and all things at the end of time (cf. 2 Cor 3:18). As Dunn says, the spirituals:

'must be set and seen within the context of the fundamental eschatological tension of Christian experience.'[2] This point is of such significance that it needs to be acknowledged in any definition of the charism of faith.

The Charism of Faith as a Gift

Later in 1 Cor 12, Paul dropped the word *pneumatika* in favour of *charisma.* He may have done this because it was associated with the miraculous spiritual gifts of Hellenism. Or it may be that the Corinthians were using the word in a boastful, elitist, and therefore divisive fashion to refer to their 'superior' gifts. As one bible scholar has written: 'Paul used the word "charism" to denote a concrete materialisation of God's grace which was neither equivalent to pneumatic phenomena, nor identical with power or service.'[3] The word *charismata* occurs fourteen times in the writings attributed to Paul. Apparently, it was not derived from Greek literature, the Septuagint or from the Christian community. In all probability, Paul borrowed the term from colloquial Greek. From an etymological point of view it is derived from *charizomai:* 'to please' and *charis:* 'grace.' So the word *charisma* could be translated as 'gift-in-grace.' *Charisma* therefore, is a concept that we owe almost entirely to St Paul, one that expresses his Christian rather than his Jewish experience. During a debate on the gifts at the Second Vatican Council, it was said: '*Charisma* for St Paul, has a very wide meaning, which also, and even especially includes services that are stable.'[4]

Many modern theologians and exegetes would endorse this understanding. By using this original theological term, Paul tried to get away from any hint of elitism that the Corinthians might have expressed with the word, *pneumatika.* Scripture scholars are also agreed that Paul did not use the word *charisma* in a technical sense to refer to extraordinary gifts of the Spirit such as healings and miracles. Instead, he used it in a much broader vocational sense, to refer to *all graced abilities,* such as hospitality, intercession, and celibacy, that edify the Christian community which is the body of Christ. Herman Ridderbos has written: 'The whole distinction between charismatic and non-charismatic ministries in the Church therefore cannot be reconciled with the Pauline conception of *charisma.*'[5] As a result, every

Christian has a charism/s (1 Cor 12:7) ranging from ordinary gifts such as administration and almsgiving, to the more extraordinary charisms such as prophecy, tongues, faith, miracle working, etc. So, rather then giving rise to rivalry or division in the community, the charisms should be employed for the common good of all.

The Charism of Faith as a Form of Service

Paul refers to charisms, such as the charism of faith, as *diakonai* or 'services.' In secular Greek the word was used to describe all kinds of labour such as waiting on tables, working for the civil authorities, collecting money for the poor, etc. Jesus had highlighted the importance of service in (Lk 22:27), and gave the example himself when he wrapped a towel about his waist and washed the disciple's feet (Jn 13:4-20). St Paul describes how Christ can be imitated when he says, 'through love be servants of one another' Gal 5:13. In 1 Cor 12 he is saying that this can be done by exercising the gifts in a loving way, including the charism of faith.

The Charism of Faith as an Energy or Power

In 1 Cor 12:6 the apostle describes the charisms as *energemata,* or 'workings.' In Greek, the word has affinities with *energeia* meaning 'energy' or 'power.' The power involved, is the power of the Holy Spirit, which raised Jesus from the dead. In Eph 1:17-20, we read: 'May he, (the Lord) enlighten the eyes of your mind so that you can see ... how extraordinarily great is the power that he has exercised for us believers; this accords with the strength of his power at work in Christ, the power which he exercised in raising him from the dead.' While this power is operative in all the charisms, it is particularly obvious in so-called deeds of power such as exorcisms, healings and miracles, which are made possible by the charism of faith, when God's divine energy is momentarily released. As St Paul reminded some of his earliest converts: 'Our gospel came to you not only in word, but also in power and the Holy Spirit and with full conviction' 1 Thess 1:5. In 1 Cor 2:4 he says in similar vein: 'my speech and my message were not in plausible words of wisdom, but in demonstration of the Spirit and power.' As he says in 1 Cor 4:20, 'The kingdom of God does not consist in talk but in power.' It is highly likely that when Paul refers to such things as 'power' and the 'demonstration of the Spirit' he has healings, miracles and exorcisms in mind.

The Charism of Faith as a Manifestation of God

In 1 Cor 12:7 Paul uses another beautiful term *phanerosis* to describe the charisms. It is particularly applicable to the charisms of power. It means 'manifestation,' or 'epiphany.' In other words, whenever the charisms are exercised, including the charism of faith, they are mini theophanies which reveal and disclose the presence of the risen Lord. There is a good example of what Paul had in mind, when he said in 1 Cor 14:24-26, that if an unbeliever came into a prayer meeting and heard a prophetic utterance that cut him to the heart: 'that person will bow down before God and worship him, declaring, "God is really among you".' One could accurately refer to an incident like this as an emmanuel experience.

Classification of the charisms

Many scripture scholars have looked at the charisms listed in 1 Cor 12:8-10, and wondered if they could be classified in terms of subject matter. It is probable that Paul had no such classification consciously in mind. Nevertheless, the charisms can be grouped in a meaningful way – on the basis of theological and experiential criteria – that can help to throw light on the charism of faith and its possible relationship to the other charisms. John Cassian (c. 365-435 A.D.) was the first to do so. He divided the charisms into three groups. In our own day a number of different groupings have been proposed. They involve either three or four headings. Actually, there is a good deal of overlap between the different suggestions. They could be grouped as follows.

A. Charisms of revelation
   i.e. wisdom, knowledge, discernment of spirits

B. Charisms of proclamation
   i.e. prophecy, tongue speaking, interpretation of tongues

C. Charisms of demonstration
   i.e., faith, healings, exorcisms and miracles.

According to this classification

There are charisms that enable the believer to know the Lord and his will.

There are other charisms that enable him or her to tell others about this good news,

There are others which manifest its reality by means of liberating deeds of power.

This is a quasi-sacramental view, where word and deed, together, conspire to make Christ present.

Finally, it is worth noting, that Paul's thinking about the charisms is situated within the wider context of his teaching about the church as the Body of Christ. In Rom 12:14-15 and 1 Cor 12:12-27, he emphasises the church's unity, even though there are varied gifts, ministries, and personalities. In Eph 4:4-12, and Col 1:18-24, Christ is recognised as head of the body the church. A passage redolent with the Pauline spirit says that the charisms were given by the Holy Spirit: '...To equip the saints for the work of ministry, for building up the body of Christ, until all of us come to the unity of the faith and of the knowledge of the Son of God, to maturity, to the measure of the full stature of Christ' Eph 4:12.

The Charism of Faith and its Associated Gifts

In the last century Herman Gunkel wrote: 'The theology of the great apostle is an expression of his experience, not of his reading ... Paul believes in the divine Spirit, because he has experienced him.'[6] So when he wrote down the list of charisms in 1 Cor 12:8-10, he did so in the light of his own experience. For example, we know from his teaching that he was endowed with the gifts of wisdom and knowledge to a remarkable degree. In 2 Cor 12:4 he says that having being caught up into Paradise: 'he heard things that cannot be told, which man may not utter.' With regard to his deeds of power Acts 19:11 says: 'And God did extraordinary miracles by the hands of Paul.' So, surely, then, there is nothing accidental about the fact that the gift of faith is preceded by the charisms of wisdom and knowledge and followed by those of healing and miracle working. It is like a keystone in a charismatic bridge. In general terms it could be said that while charismatic faith depends on the gifts of wisdom and knowledge it leads to the gifts of healing and miracle working. Before looking at charismatic faith we will look briefly at its companion gifts.

Scripture scholars maintain that there is a lot of overlap between the gifts of wisdom and knowledge. As result they are hard to separate. However, in the light of other New Testament and Old Testament texts, exegetes try to describe the complementary characteristics of each gift. The gifts of wisdom and knowledge are mentioned in Is 11:2, and again in 1 Cor 12:8. Many scholars agree that the gifts mentioned by Isaiah are sanctifying graces, whereas the charisms of the *utterance* of wisdom and the *utterance* of knowledge mentioned by Paul, e.g. in the form of anointed preaching and teaching, are gratuitous graces.[7] They are given for the edification of others and are not necessarily indications that the one who exercises them is holy. Indeed St Thomas Aquinas believed that a person in a state of mortal sin could exercise a charism of power such as healing.

The Gift of Wisdom. It is practical rather than speculative. There is a prayer asking for such wisdom in Col 1:9, 'We have never failed to remember you in our prayers and ask that through perfect wisdom and spiritual understanding you should reach the fullest understanding of his will.' As Montague explains, the word of wisdom: 'Would seem to refer to a special insight given in a transient way by the Holy Spirit to an individual or community by way of a directive or a counsel on how best to live the Christian life.'[8]

The Gift of Knowledge. It has two main aspects. Firstly, it can refer to an inspired understanding of God's word and the Christian mysteries. For example, the scriptures, especially the New Testament, abounds in divine promises. They are to do with salvation; God's willingness to help people in their difficulties; and the assurance of eventual resurrection. God's word of promise can be understood in two different ways.

Firstly, there is the inspired word of promise as a *noun*, which is objectively true in itself in general terms. Secondly, there is the inspired and inspiring message of promise as a *verb*, which is subjectively true for the hearer in his or her particular circumstances. It is this 'alive and active,' word of knowledge, that evokes the confidence and inner certitude that God will do what has been promised.

The second way in which Paul seems to understand the word of knowledge is that it is an inspired awareness of a fact about a person or an event. Jesus often exercised this gift, e.g. when he told the Samaritan woman about the fact that there were five men in her life (Jn 4:18). It also seems to be operative in the story of the conversion of Cornelius and his household by St Peter. Both men were brought together by inspired words of knowledge (Acts 10). Well known twentieth century 'charismatics' such as Padre Pio, Kathryn Kulhman, Emeliano Tardiff, Briege McKenna and John Wimber[9] claim that they exercise this gift. The validly of their claims seems to be endorsed by the well attested healings that are regularly associated with their ministries.

The Gift of Healings. If the charism of faith depends on the gifts of wisdom and knowledge it is expressed by means of the gift of healings. Paul is not referring to medical healing, but rather to a Spirit given ability to heal in the way that Jesus did. It is quite likely that the notion of exorcism is included in the charism of healings. It is worth noting that in the Greek of the New Testament, Paul talks about the gift in the plural (cf. 1 Cor 12:10; 28; 29). The use of the plural can be interpreted in different ways. Firstly, it may be that Paul recognised that one person in the community might be able to heal one particular kind of sickness, e.g. bad backs, while others might be able to heal other ailments such as deafness, skin disease, depression, etc. In that sense there would be different but complementary gifts of healing in the church. Secondly, Paul may have been referring to the fact that many people exercise the gift of healing, in that sense there is a gift of healings. Thirdly, Paul may have been suggesting that the gift of healing is ephemeral rather than permanent. As such, it is new each time it is exercised. I suspect that this latter interpretation is the correct one.

The Gift of Working Miracles. The charism of faith which depends on the gifts of wisdom and knowledge can also be expressed by means of miracle working. Once again Paul uses the plural. The gift of miracles, or *dunameis* i.e. 'deeds of power' in Greek, can be variously translated as 'the working of miracles,' or as 'operations of works of power.' In biblical terms a miracle is a marvel or sign that evokes astonishment. In all probability it wouldn't include the contemporary Western notion of a miracle as an event that goes beyond the laws of nature as they are presently understood. Paul may be referring to nature miracles (cf. Acts 16:26; 28:3f). Like Jesus both he and the other apostles performed marvellous deeds, e.g. Peter raised Dorcas to life (Acts 9:40), Paul raised Eutychus (Acts 20:10) and in Gal 3:5 the apostle speaks about the way God 'works miracles among you.'

The Charism of Faith. The question we need to address at this point is, what did Paul mean when he spoke about the charism of faith in 1 Cor 12:9? While he says very little about it directly, a careful examination of relevant texts enables us to infer what he might have had in mind. When he talks about the charism of faith he presupposes that the person adheres to the Christian creed, has been justified by faith, and that he or she has faith as a fruit of the Spirit. Clearly Paul has another kind of faith in mind here. Well known exegetes are all agreed on this point.[10] Montague is representative of their shared opinion when he writes: 'The gift of faith does not refer here to the faith that is necessary for salvation (Mk 16:16; Heb 11:6), but rather to a special intensity of faith for a specific need.[11] In *A Greek English Lexicon of the New Testament* we read: 'In addition to the faith that every Christian possesses Paul speaks of a special gift of faith that is the possession of a select few (cf 1 Cor 12:9). In this category he understands faith as an unquestioning belief in God's power to aid men with miracles, the faith that 'moves mountains.' This special kind of faith is what the disciples had in mind when they asked 'increase our faith' Lk 17:5.[12]

Incidentally, the scholars are also agreed that, it is highly likely that the charismatic faith Paul has in mind is referred to again in 1 Cor 13:2 when he says, 'though I have *all the faith to move mountains* - if I am without love I am nothing.' It seems to be a kind of openness and confidence that enables the power of God to operate through the person who has it.[13] Many well known scripture scholars endorse this understanding. James Dunn says: 'Paul presumably has in mind that mysterious *surge of confidence* which sometimes arises within a man in a particular situation of need or challenge and which gives him an unusual certainty and assurance that God is about to act through a word or through an action.'[14] F. Pratt concurs: 'The charism of faith is an *invincible confidence*, founded on theological faith, and assured by a supernatural instinct, that God in a given case, will manifest his power, his justice, or his mercy.'[15] Ridderbos, adds that the charism of faith is a form of exceptional trust which is granted to some people. It enables them to believe in a real as opposed to a notional way, that 'with God all things are possible' Mt 19:26. He adds by way of explanation: 'With this *charisma* it is accordingly not only a question of certainty of what God will do in his time and way in the fulfilling of his promises, but of a certainty of being enabled by God at a specific moment to perform a miracle.'[16]

It is noticeable that there is a recurrent theme in the scholarly comments on the charism of faith. They refer variously to, 'confidence,' 'a question of certainty,' and 'complete and unshakable trust.' These points were encapsulated by Catholic theologian Joseph Brosch before the Second Vatican Council. He defined charismatic faith as: 'A supernatural ability to discern with *conviction* that God is going to reveal his power, righteousness and mercy in a very definitive concrete case.' He went on to add these cautionary words: 'Should another person who does not have the charism, wish to induce a similar miracle of God, in such a case, one would have to say, "he is tempting God" ... The gift of faith is nothing less than *fides miraculosa,* the power of the Holy Spirit manifested in order to accomplish the will of God despite all natural resistance, and above all, the power to triumph over a world at enmity with God.'[17]

Where does this subjective sense of certainty and conviction come from? Some scholars say that it is rooted in an inspired understanding of God's will which is made possible by the gifts of wisdom and knowledge. What is involved here is not so much a knowledge of the mysteries of the Christian religion, – although it can include it – as an experiential, contemplative awareness of God, and God's benevolent purposes. It is this objective knowledge of an inspired and illuminating kind, that evokes the subjective state of personal conviction. While one can choose, under the impulse of grace, to seek God and God's will, it is worth noting that the state of inner conviction characteristic of the charism of faith, is *evoked* by the inspired knowledge of the Lord, and *not directly willed*. This is a fundamental point as far as the Pauline understanding of the charism of faith is concerned.

The Charism of Faith Defined

In the light of what has been said so far, the gift of faith can be defined as follows.

> The charism of faith refers to a special grace, given to some, by the Holy Spirit, which enables them in particular situations, to discern with convinced and expectant faith of a heartfelt kind, that God will manifest his unconditional mercy and love as a sign of the transformation of all things in the end times, through a deed of power, such as a healing, exorcism or miracle.

The charism can be expressed as follows in analytical terms:

1. The charism of faith is a special grace, that is given to *some* by the Spirit in order to perform an act of service.
2. It is not a gift for all situations in general, it operates in concrete and *particular* situations.
3. It is rooted in the discernment of *God's will*, by means of the gifts of wisdom or knowledge
4. Knowledge of God and God's will leads to the heartfelt conviction, and trustful *expectation* that God is beginning to act in the present or will act in the future.
5. God's mercy and love are mainly manifested in a *deed of power* such as a healing, exorcism and miracle working.
6. Such deeds of power are intimations and anticipations in the present of the *transformation* of all things in the Second Coming.

Gifts and Ministries

In Pauline theology there was not only a complementarity between the charisms, e.g. in 1 Cor 12:8-10, there was also a corresponding complementarity between the ministries, such as bishop, deacon, apostle, evangelist, teacher, prophet, and shepherd (cf. Eph 4:11-16). Although charisms and ministries were often interrelated they were separate.[18] A ministry was an office received by delegation and exercised with authority.[19] Ultimately the authority came from Jesus Christ and was animated by the Spirit. The Christian community had to discern who had what ministry. Then it had to encourage the gifted person to engage in his or her particular form of service for the good of all. More often than not, a person who had received a ministry would also receive charisms that would help him or her to exercise it effectively. For example, a teacher might have the charisms of wisdom and knowledge. Apostles and evangelists, however, were the people who were most likely to receive the charism of faith and its accompanying gifts of healing and miracle working. As a result they were be able to demonstrate the truth of the good news they preached by means of deeds of power. As Paul said in Rom 15:18-19, 'I will venture to speak only of what Christ has done through me to win obedience from the Gentiles, by word and deed, by the power of signs and wonders, by the power of the Spirit of God.'

Problematic References to the Charism of Faith

At this juncture, the focus changes to three Pauline texts, 2 Cor 8:7 and Rom 12:3; 6, because, in his book *Jesus and the Spirit*, James Dunn maintains that they refer to the charism of faith.[20] The aim here is, firstly, to examine each of the nominated texts in the light of the definition above in order to establish whether they are genuine references to charismatic faith or not. The second aim, is to see whether the definition might need to be modified in the light of other references to the charism of faith.

1) In 2 Cor 8:7, Paul writes: 'You are so rich in everything – in *faith*, speech, knowledge, and diligence of every kind, as well as in the love you have for us.' Dunn, believes that this verse probably refers to charismatic faith. In his commentary, Furnish offers the same interpretation.[21] He thinks that the speech Paul is referring to, is firstly, a charismatic type utterance of knowledge which is rooted in inspired insight (cf. 1 Cor 12:8); and secondly, that the faith he mentions is the gift of inner certainty which can inform such utterances just as it can inform healings and miracle working. If this interpreta-

tion is correct, we have once again the connection between inspired knowledge, charismatic faith and deeds of power.

2) Attention shifts now to two similar texts. In Rom 12:3 Paul says, 'Do not think too highly of yourself, but form a sober estimate based on the *measure of faith* that God has dealt to each of you.' In Rom 12:6 he adds; 'Let us use the different gifts allotted to each of us by God's grace; the gift of utterance, for example, let us use *in proportion to our faith.*' Dunn says that when Paul mentions the 'measure' or 'proportion' of faith he is referring to its charismatic form, rather than faith of a justifying kind.[22] He maintains that the two phrases refer to the ensuing list of gifts in Rom 12:6-9. Then he goes on to add that the phrase 'the measure of faith' is used in a similar way in Eph 4:7. Both imply a consciousness of being gratuitously empowered by God in a particular situation. Faith can, therefore, act as a measure, one that is determined by the degree of one's inner confidence or certitude: 'precisely because it is *that assurance* that God is speaking or acting through the charismatic's words or actions.'[23]

Is Dunn's evaluation of these texts correct? There are a number of reasons for questioning its validity. In an authoritative commentary on Romans Fitzmyer asserts that Rom 12:3 does not refer to the charism of faith.[24] He says that the word *'faith'* refers either to the active response of the believer to the truths of faith (subjective conviction) or to the dogma believed (objective truth). It is also questionable whether Paul is referring to the charism of faith in Rom 12:6. In this instance Fitzmyer suggests that there are three possible ways of interpreting the verse.[25] Firstly, the word 'faith,' may refer to the Christian creed. There are linguistic clues that suggest that may be the correct view. The literal translation of the Greek in verse six reads, 'If prophecy, according to the proportion of the faith.' The word *analogia* can mean 'proportion,' 'measure,' or 'rule.' The use of the definite article suggests that the word 'faith' is being used in an objective sense. In other words, when a prophet speaks, he or she should only say things in conformity with the Christian creed. If this interpretation is correct, says Montague in another commentary, then verse six could be translated as follows, 'If your gift is prophecy, use it according to the norms set by the faith.'[26] Significantly, Bultmann agrees with this interpretation.[27] Secondly, the word 'faith' in verse six, may refer to the person's subjective experience of faith, in other words, inspired speaking should only be engaged in, in accordance with the inner awareness of grace. Thirdly, the word 'faith' could possibly apply to the charism mentioned in 1 Cor 12:9. If so then it would mean, that if by a prophetic word one has an ability to move mountains, it should be truly inspired, and unsullied by any self-centred concerns. Although Fitzmyer mentions these possibilities, he doesn't commit himself to any of them. On the balance, however it seems unlikely that either Rom 12:3 or 12:6 refer to the charism of faith.

Faith Through Love

Finally, 1 Cor 13:2, St Paul makes it clear that the charism of faith, has no real significance unless it is the expression of the love of God, which is unrestricted and unconditional in nature. This is the highest and greatest of all the spiritual gifts. The charism of faith, therefore, should be rooted in love, express that love, and aim to build up the same love in the Christian community, the body of Christ. As Paul says in Gal 5:6, it is a matter of 'faith working through love.' While the word 'faith' here, refers primarily to justifying faith, it can in a secondary and dependent way, refer to the charism of faith. So according to Paul, even if a person exercises the charism of faith and moves a mountain, he or she will nevertheless, be accounted as nothing unless he or she is motivated by divine love (1 Cor 13:2).

This chapter indicated that while the charism of faith in 1 Cor 12:9;13:2 is related to other forms of faith it is nevertheless distinct from them. As a supernatural gift of God, the charism of faith, like the other charisms listed in 1 Cor 12:8-10, is a form of service whereby the love of God is manifested by the power of God. It was suggested that the charism of faith is rooted in inspired knowledge, by means of the gifts of wisdom and knowledge, and expressed in and through deeds of power such as healings and miracle working. On this basis a definition of the charism of faith was proposed, one that involved six characteristic elements. The most important of these is the inner sense of certainty that is evoked by an inspired, intuitive awareness of God's purposes. Some problematic texts were examined to see if they referred to the charism of faith or not. It is possible that Rom 12:3 and Rom 12:6 refer to expectant faith of the unhesitating kind, but it is less likely that 2 Cor 8:7 does so.

CHAPTER FOUR

Was Jesus an Exemplar of Unhesitating Faith?

Scripture scholars and theologians alike, are agreed that after his baptism in the Jordan, Jesus exercised a number of charisms, including those of healing, exorcism and miracle working. This gives rise to an important and specific question. Besides being the object of faith, did Jesus exercise the charism of faith? Four points need to be considered in order to come to a tentative conclusion. Firstly, some introductory observations will be made about kenotic Christology, i.e. the way Jesus emptied himself of divine glory, because it has implications for the general approach of this chapter. Secondly, there will be an examination of key texts in the letters attributed to Paul. It will aim to establish whether Jesus is referred to as a man of faith or not. Thirdly, a number of key passages in the Synoptics will also be studied in order to establish whether they refer to the faith of Jesus, and the charism of faith in particular. Fourthly, the contention that Jesus was a man of faith has a theological dimension, so it is important to take a critical look – albeit a brief one – at what traditional and contemporary scholarship has to say about this important issue.

The Kenotic Christ

We begin with the *kenotic* passage in Phil 2:6-9, because it makes a general theological point. The way in which it is understood has a bearing on the way in which other relevant texts, to do with the possible faith of Jesus, can be interpreted. In this well known Christological hymn, which he may have borrowed from the liturgy of his day, Paul tells us that Jesus, 'did not count equality with God something to be grasped, but he emptied himself ... becoming as human beings are; and *being in every way like a human being*' Phil 2:7.

The word 'emptied' is a powerful one. In the incarnation, the

Son of God, emptied himself of his 'deity to take upon himself his humanity,' says Barclay in his commentary on this passage.[1] Perhaps it would be more accurate to say that rather than emptying himself of his divinity, Jesus emptied himself of all the privileges and prerogatives of divinity, to take on the appearance or form of a human being and a slave. How radical was this *kenosis*? In Heb 4:5 we read: 'we have one who *in every respect* has been tested as we are, yet without sin.' 2 Cor 5:21 goes so far as to say that, 'For our sake he made him to be sin who knew no sin.' In other words, Jesus seems to have suffered some of the effects of sin, such as a certain feeling of distance from God. F. X. Durwell has written: 'Christ began by entering into our wretchedness himself; he shared with man that existence which Scripture calls existence according to the flesh. A natural existence not animated by the glorious holiness of God ... He was still the Son of God. *But there were within him quite considerable elements which God's glorifying holiness did not enter*; not only his body, but all the faculties which brought him into contact with us, were so incompletely possessed by the life of God that Christ could suffer fear and anguish, and the Son of the immortal God could succumb to death.'[2]

According to the evangelists the *kenotic* Jesus was utterly dependent in all things upon God, his Father. For instance he was led by the Spirit (cf. Lk 4:1). Jesus testified that God revealed to him what to say, what to do, and how to do it (cf. Jn 8:28; 12:50; 5:19). At the end of his life, when he faced his supreme crucifixion point of powerlessness, he committed his life in a spirit of obedience and trust (cf. Lk 23:46) into the hands of him 'who was able to save him from death' Heb 5:7. The question arises, if Jesus was human like us in every respect, except sin, did he, like us, have faith in the God of the promises and in the promises of God? And if so, what kind of faith was it?

Dunn reflects the view of a majority of scripture scholars when he says, that although there are many passages where Jesus encourages people to have faith, commends them when it is present, and rebukes them when it is absent, 'none of these passages speaks of the faith *of* Jesus.'[3] Bultmann expressed the same point of view when he wrote: 'The Gospels do not speak of Jesus' own faith, nor does the kerygma make reference to it.'[4]

That said, there are reasons – as Ebeling and others have pointed out[5] – for seeing Jesus as a 'witness of faith,' i.e. one whose life disclosed the fact that he, like others before and after him, exercised trust in God. It is ironic, in view of Dunn's statement above, that commenting on the charism of faith he says that is a mysterious surge of confidence which sometimes arises within a person and which gives him an unusual certainty and assurance that God is about to act. Then he adds '*Jesus certainly knew such experiences.*'[6] Catholic theologian John Sobrino would agree that Jesus is the model of faith filled discipleship: 'The most radical and most orthodox affirmation of *faith in Jesus* is affirming that the *faith of Jesus* is the correct way to draw nearer to God and realise his kingdom, and then acting accordingly.'[7]

The Faith of Jesus in the Letters of Paul

Since the 19th century, scripture scholars have argued, inconclusively, about the proper translation of seven verses in the letters of Paul, i.e. Rom 3:22; 3:26; Gal 2.16a; 2:16b; 2:20; 3:22; Phil 3:9. They are important because they may refer to the faith of Jesus. In each a genitive occurs. However it is not clear whether they should be translated as objective genitives which refer to the faith of the believer, or subjective genitives which would refer to the faith of Jesus. There is no need to look at them in detail. Suffice it to say, that Wallis has argued on grammatical, scriptural and theological grounds, that all of them can legitimately be translated as subjective genitives. As such they can be seen as points on a theological curve that refers to the faith of Jesus Christ.[8]

In Rom 3:21-22, for example, St Paul writes, 'But now, apart from law, the righteousness of God has been disclosed, and is attested by the law and the prophets, the righteousness of God through faith in Jesus Christ for all who believe.' The phrase 'faith in Jesus Christ' can be translated as 'through the faith *of* Jesus Christ.' However, after a careful evaluation of the pros and cons, Fitzmyer, says that although the Greek can be translated as 'the faith *of* Jesus Christ,' or 'the fidelity *of* Jesus Christ,' it is unlikely that this is what Paul had in mind, because it runs counter to the general thrust of his theology.[9] To support his case Fitzmyer says that Paul does not draw attention to Christ's faith or fidelity in the rest of Romans. For example, although chapter four depicts Abraham as a model of faith, there is no mention of the faith of Christ. That said, it is possible that Rom 3:21-22, like the other references could possibly refer to the faith of Jesus. Wallis argues that when taken together, 'there are substantial grounds for maintaining that in each case Paul had Christ's own faith in mind.'[10]

There are a number of references in the deutero-Pauline epistles, i.e. letters that may have been written by disciples of Paul. They occur in Eph 3:12; 1 Tim 1:14; 3:13; 2 Tim 1:13; 2 Tim 3:15. Again, because of the ambiguity of the Greek, they can be translated in such a way that they could refer to the faith of Christ. Here is a typical example. The author of 1 Tim 1:14 says: 'The grace of our Lord overflowed for me with the faith and love that are in Christ Jesus.' Although this text could be referring to the believer's faith in Christ, it can be understood as a reference to the faith *of* Christ. The emphasis here, however, is different from the Pauline one. Whereas the apostle sees the faith of Christ in relation to the way in which salvation is made available through the cross, the pastoral epistles see his faith from the point of view of the believer making appropriate responses to the grace of salvation.

The third group of texts to be examined includes Heb 2:17; 3:2;6; 12:2; Rev 1:5;3; 14; 19:11. Again these are chosen because, they can be read as explicit or implicit references to the faith of Jesus. For example, Heb 12:2 is an important verse because it contains one of the clearest references. In some editions of the Bible it has been translated as, 'Let us run with perseverance the race that is set before us, looking to Jesus the pioneer and perfecter of *our* faith.' In other editions however it is translated, 'run with resolution the race which lies ahead of us, our eyes fixed on Jesus, the pioneer and perfecter *of faith*.' When the verse is read, in the Greek, it becomes clear that the latter translation is the accurate one from a linguistic point of view. As a result, the phrase 'perfecter of faith' could refer either to our faith in Jesus, the faith of Jesus himself, or possibly both together. Attridge advocates this latter position, in his commentary, when he writes: 'It is neither Christ himself nor his followers … that are perfected, but the faith that both share.'[11]

There is no clinching argument that would help us to come down decidedly in favour of one or other of the options. Suffice it to say that, it is not unreasonable to maintain that Heb 12:2 refers to the faith of Jesus. In 'Faith in the Epistle to the Hebrews: The Jesus Factor,' Dennis Hamm, agrees with fellow scholars Wescott, Attridge, Hughes, and Vanhoye, who say that in Hebrews Jesus is not only an enabler of faith but also its model and exemplar.[12] Wallis endorses this conclusion when he says that Jesus 'is portrayed as the believer *par excellence*.'[13]

The Faith of Jesus in the Synoptics.

It seems that it would be reasonable to say, having briefly examined the texts in the previous section, that there are sufficient, but not conclusive, grounds for believing that they refer to the faith of Jesus. This section will look at key passages in the synoptics in order to ask the question, are there good reasons for believing that they refer to the faith of Jesus and specifically, to his exercise of the charism of faith?

Before looking at specific scripture texts, there is one general point to be made. Consistent with a kenotic perspective, we can usefully look at the writings of Geza Vermes. He has pointed out, from a Jewish point of view, that, in terms of the Judaism of his day, Jesus was a charismatic holy man in the tradition of Elijah and Elisha, both of whom were miracle-working prophets. He was also similar to the *Hasidim* or The Devout, i.e. holy men, such as Honi the Circle-Drawer (1st cent. B.C.) and Hanina ben Dosa (1st cent. A.D.) whose prayer was believed to be all powerful and capable of working miracles. The latter is reputed to have said, 'he whose actions exceed his wisdom, his wisdom shall endure, but he whose wisdom exceeds his actions, his wisdom shall not endure.'[14]

For example, Hanina, chose to live a life of poverty. It is said that when the son of the famous Gamaliel was ill, the head of the Jerusalem Pharisees sent two of his pupils to implore Hanina's prayers. The holy man retired to an upper room, prayed fervently, and returned with the words, 'go home, for the fever has departed from him.' The two young men were so surprised they asked, incredulously, 'Are you a prophet?' to which Hanina replied, 'I am no prophet, nor am I a prophet's son, but this is how I am favoured. If my prayer is fluent in my mouth, I know that the sick man is favoured; if not, I know that the disease is fatal.'[15] When the pupils returned to their teacher they found that Gamaliel's son had recovered at the very hour that Hanina had prayed. The phrase, 'if my prayer is fluent in my mouth,' is an intriguing one. It seems to imply, a rapport with God's will and an inner conviction or certainty that the prayer is being answered, which are characteristics of the charism of faith.

We read of similar incidents in the life of Jesus. This would imply that because of his self-emptying, he may have been like the *Hasidim* in the way he prayed and performed deeds of power. When Jesus met with needy people, e.g. the man with a virulent skin-disease in Mk 1:40-45, he appears to have had a characteristic way of ministering to them. Firstly, he felt compassion, which was a participation in, and a revelation of, the loving kindness of the heart of his Father. Secondly, in the light of that compassionate love he was led in a prayerful way by the Spirit, (Mt 4:1) to see, by means of the gifts of wisdom and knowledge, what the Father was doing (Jn 5:19). Thirdly, having discerned God's will, it seems that he was inwardly certain that the Lord was authorising and empowering him to minister to the afflicted person. In other words Jesus had the trusting conviction which is typical of the charism of faith. Fourthly, Unlike Hellenist or Jewish healers, he usually looked for faith in the person/s he was ministering to. If they were possessed, unconscious or dead, he looked for faith in their relatives or friends. Fifthly, he spoke a word of command and usually performed some gesture, such as the laying on of hands, and power went out of him to heal the sick person (Mk 5:30).

At this stage, we can try to answer our question from a specifically Christian point of view. Wallis is correct when he says that there are no unambiguous references to the faith of Jesus in the gospels. That said, however, there are four relevant texts worthy of examination in the synoptics. They are being chosen because each one demonstrates, as Wallis says, 'a level of correspondence between Jesus' conduct and the intended conduct of his disciples that invites comparison.'[16] There are other scholars who, by and large, support this point of view.

A) The Healing of the Epileptic boy

The first is about the healing of an epileptic boy who was presumed to be possessed. The version in Mk 9:14-29 is by far the longest. Eduard Schweitzer thinks that this is the most significant reference to faith in Mark's gospel.[17] This is a debatable judgment, in view of the fact that there is such an important passage about faith in Mk 11:20-26. In any case Mk 9:14-29 is about: (i) the nascent faith of the father of the boy, who is a suppliant, (ii) the unbelief and failure of the disciples, (iii) the faith of Jesus himself (iv) what Jesus said about the prayer of faith. Marshall points out that this passage has a four-fold scenic structure.[18] All but one of the scenes is associated with a question asked by someone – often by Jesus himself – which is followed by a declaration by the Lord.

Scene one is to do with Jesus and the crowd (vv 14-20). Jesus asks the disciples the question, 'What were you discussing with them?' They explain, and when he hears how they were unable to help the disturbed child, he responds, 'O faithless generation! How long am I to be with you? How long am I to bear with you?' The word for 'faithless' in Greek is *apistos* , which literally means 'without trust', i.e. in God or in God's power. Marshall points out that these words are primarily addressed to the disciples. Jesus is lamenting the fact that they are as unbelieving as the scribes and the crowd. He says: 'The failure of Jesus' own followers provokes in him a sense of near despair at the obduracy of unbelief in the entire contemporary generation that expresses itself in all who are present, including the father.'[19]

The second scene focuses on the relationship of Jesus with the father. Jesus asks him the question, 'How long has this been going on?' When he hears the answer, he declares, 'All things are possible to the one who believes.' The phrase 'the *one* who believes' is ambiguous in the Greek. It can refer to either the petitioner – in this case the father of the epileptic boy – or to Jesus himself. Marshall says that the preceding context, i.e. the inability of the disciples to cure the boy due to lack of faith, makes Jesus the logical focus of the phrase. In contrast, to the disciples, he has the unbounded faith to drive out the evil spirit. Marshall says, that, in spite of the fact that this is the only reference to the faith of Jesus in Mark, many commentators support this interpretation, e.g. Nineham, Schweitzer, Klostermann and Jeremias. He says that instead of being linguistically careless as some have alleged, Mark's ambiguity is intentional. He is stating that the faith of those who seek healings or miracles (in this case the father of the boy), or the faith of those who minister (in this case the disciples and then Jesus himself), is important. As Grundmann observes: 'The miracles presuppose the faith of the One who performs them and also the one on whom they are performed. They are accomplished in a wholly personal relationship.'[20] Jeremias says something similar: 'Jesus (is) at the same time depicted both as the believer who *has* blind confidence, coupled with complete surrender to God, and as the one who *summons* others to believe.'[21] If this is the case, then it is through the faith of Jesus that God's power is manifested in the exorcism.

Clearly the father of the boy is aware that Jesus is compassionate and willing to help i.e. he has a rudimentary knowledge of the Lord. Although he has real trust, it is relatively weak, as was noted already. When he hears Jesus say, 'All things are possible to him who believes' this revelatory word evokes a new depth of faith in him (cf. Rom 10:17) and he declares in a paradoxical way, 'I do have faith, Help the little faith I have.' His faith as a petitioner – the honest acknowledgment of unbelief indicates that he did not have the charism of faith – is 'rewarded' so to speak when Jesus drives out the demon with a word of command. Marshall says, that the reference to 'unbelief' is intended to show that in Mark's theology there is a tension between faith and un-faith in every believer, and that it is only by the grace of God that expectant faith of the unhesitating kind is possible.

The third scene is about Jesus and the demon. There is no question here. Jesus simply declares 'You deaf and dumb spirit. I command you, come out of him and never enter him again.' Jesus has strong and certain faith in God his Father that is expressed in a word of authority and results in a deed of power. This sequence, which conforms to the definition of the charism of faith in chapter three, suggests in a very convincing way that Jesus was exercising the charism of faith in this instance. Wallis concurs when he says: 'The means by which Jesus performs this miracle are remarkably consistent with certain characteristics of mountain moving faith spoken of elsewhere (Mt 17:20; 21:20; Mk 11:23; cf. Lk 17:6).'[22] By implication, he expected the father of the boy and also the disciples and perhaps the people in the crowd, to share in his unflinching faith. As Marshall says: 'The father is being implicitly called to emulate the faith of Jesus. And it is the faith of both parties that permits success.'[23]

Marshall says that in Mark's Gospel there are two kinds of interrelated faith, kerygmatic and petitionary. The latter can take the form of a request for oneself or another. The father asks for help for his son. That is the prelude to Jesus' faith-filled word of command. Speaking about the relationship of petition and miracle working Marshall writes: 'There is the faith required of those who seek to effect miracles. Such mountain moving faith (11:23) may express itself in a direct word of command but Mark stresses the role of petitionary prayer as the source of prayer's power.'[24] The clear implication of these comments, is that Jesus exercised the charism of faith.

The fourth scene involves Jesus and the disciples. They ask the question, 'why could we not cast it (i.e. the demon) out?' Jesus declares, 'This kind cannot be driven out by anything but prayer' (some translations add, 'and fasting'). What kind of prayer has Jesus in mind? The prayer of petition, and/or the prayer of command? Probably both. In Mk 11:23-24, the two are closely associated. Jesus firstly talks about commanding a mountain to be cast into the sea, and immediately talks about the power of faith-filled petitionary prayer. The next chapter will indicate how both kinds of prayer, involve the charism of faith. Incidentally, the need for fasting in Mk 9:29, is analogous to the need for forgiveness, which is mentioned in Mk 11:25.

B) Jesus Stills the Storm

The account of the stilling of the storm and walking on the water is recounted in a number of gospel texts. In chapter five it will be examined from the point of view of Jesus' teaching on charismatic faith. In this chapter it is worth asking, did Jesus exercise the charism of faith when he stilled the storm and walked on the water? Wallis believes that as it is recounted, the way in which Jesus stilled the storm is consistent with the mountain-moving faith spoken of in other places in the gospel (Mt 17:20; 21:20; Mk

11:23; cf. Lk 17:6).[25] Later on in the same story, the implication of Peter's ability to walk on water by the charism of faith, is that Jesus was successful for the same reason. Wallis observes that by exhibiting this kind of faith which the disciples lacked, Jesus provided the early church with another example of faith-in-action. He writes: 'A disciple must follow Jesus' example in the life of faith; but even where faith comes to expression in performatory miracle working conduct, its source and object is still the person of Jesus who is messiah, Lord and son of God.'[26]

C) Jesus curses the Fig tree

The account of the withering of the fig tree is mentioned in the first two gospels (Mt 21:18-22; Mk 11:12-14;20-25). Once again, the question can be asked, did Jesus exercise the charism of faith when he cursed the fig tree? A reading of the text implies that Jesus had indeed exercised that kind of faith when he successfully cursed the fig tree. Wallis comments: 'Jesus who renders the fig tree barren by faith, explains the nature of that faith to his disciples and uses his own example as a means of encouraging them to perform similar and more far reaching miracles.'[27]

D) Other relevant texts

There are other debatable references to the faith of Jesus which give reason to think that Jesus practiced what he preached, namely, a firm and certain trust in God. His prayer seems, on occasion, to express that deep trust, e.g. thanking God in anticipation of the raising of Lazarus, 'Father, I thank you for hearing my prayer, I myself know that you hear me always' Jn 11:41-42. The prayer of thanksgiving, in the Greek, refers to completed past actions. In other words, Jesus is recalling with gratitude, the times when the Father has performed deeds of power through him. This notion of anticipatory gratitude, based on present conviction of an inspired kind, is mentioned in Phil 4:6; 'The Lord is near. Do not worry about anything, but in everything by prayer and supplication *with thanksgiving* let your requests be made known to God.' This prayer, is full of the conviction Jesus spoke about in Mk 11:24. It is a matter of present conviction rather than conditional hope for the future. This accords with point four of the analytical definition of the charism of faith in chapter three.

There is also evidence of this kind of faith in Jesus' *amen* sayings, his conviction that Jairus's daughter would be restored to life, and the unquestioning reliance he placed on the Father 'who was able to save him from death' Heb 5:7. So, although Jesus didn't need justifying faith because of his sinlessness and intimate union with the Father, there is support in the synoptic gospels, for the contention that as God's faithful servant he placed his trust in God, and exercised the charism of faith in his many deeds of power. These miracles demonstrated the truth of the good news of salvation, authenticated his unique role, and they illustrated the importance of the charism of faith in the life of a disciple.

The faith of Jesus: A Theological Perspective

In Christian theology there is the doctrine of Christ's two natures. One is human, the other divine. The point is relevant here. When his humanity is emphasised, Jesus appears to be a man of great faith. We have noted how an increasing number of scripture scholars adopt this position. There are also quotations in the writings of the Fathers of the Church which seem to talk about the faith of Jesus. For example, Tertullian wrote a polemical work which challenged the Docetists who denied that Jesus was truly human. He said in an ambiguous phrase: 'Christ however, could not have appeared among men except as a man. Restore therefore, to Christ his faith.'[28] Perhaps Tertullian was saying, 'restore to Christ the faith which is his due,' or 'restore to Christ the fact that, as a man, he had faith.' Hillary of Poitiers d. 368 A.D., maintained in a less unambiguous statement that: 'For us the one true faith concerning God is that of which he is at once the Author and the *Witness*.'[29] Gregory of Nyssa d. 394 A.D., observed in a comment which has the ambiguity of Heb 12:2, that: 'We may learn the same truth from Paul, when he says that Jesus was made an Apostle and High Priest by God, being faithful to him that made Him so.'[30]

When his divinity is emphasised, Jesus is seen as someone who interiorly enjoyed the beatific vision and who therefore had no need of faith. Like St Athanasius d. 373 A.D. before him, St Thomas wrote: 'From the very moment of his conception Christ had the full vision of the very being of God, as we will hold later on. *Therefore he could not have had faith.*'[31] This was the prevailing view in the Middle Ages and it has continued right down to our own day. The knowledge of Jesus is a central one in this debate. Whereas some modern Christologies argue that Jesus had to learn like the rest of us, most traditional Christologies have maintained that besides his experimental human knowledge, Jesus enjoyed a certain omniscience in virtue of his divine status.

From a Catholic perspective, this point of view has found authoritative endorsement in Pius XII's *Mystici Corporis* (1943). It affirmed that, right from his mother's womb, Christ's human intellect was informed by the beatific vision. As a result he knew all future members of the church. On the other hand one could believe, that in virtue of his *kenosis* Jesus had limited and imperfect knowledge. Theologians, Collins and Kendall argue persuasively that there are good reasons for believing this. While they accept that Jesus was aware of who he was as Son of God, and his divine mission, they raise six objections to the notion of the beatific vision and its consequent omniscience.

Firstly, how could Jesus really suffer if he enjoyed the beatific vision?

Secondly, the notion of beatific vision is not very compatible with human freedom which is usually constrained by limited knowledge.

Thirdly, his trials and temptations would have been seriously compromised by the beatific vision.

Fourthly, St Thomas's notion of Jesus' comprehensive knowledge of creatures, seems to be incompatible with the dynamics and limitations of human knowing.

Fifthly, the synoptics imply that there were indeed limitations to the knowledge of Jesus, e.g. Mk 5:30-32; 13:32.

Sixthly, the notion of omniscience seems to compromise the notion of true humanity.[32]

Speaking about this final point, John Macquarrie says that a belief in the omniscience of Christ: 'would be utterly subversive of the true humanity of Christ.'[33] Raymond Brown adds, 'if theologians should ultimately come to accept the limitations of Jesus' knowledge that we have seen reflected *prima facie* in the biblical evidence, then how much more shall we understand that God so loved us that he subjected himself to our most agonising infirmities.'[34] He points out that some of the Church Fathers believed that Jesus was not omniscient. For example, St Cyril of Alexandria wrote: 'We have admired Christ's Goodness in that for love of us he had not refused to descend to such a low position as to bear all that belongs to our nature, included in which is ignorance.'[35] In the light of this quotation, it would be more likely that Jesus needed faith, whereas if he knew all things, such faith would not have been necessary.

A point that is overlooked in most studies of the faith of Jesus, is the distinction between the different forms of faith. Once they are acknowledged, the question about whether Jesus had faith or not, can be answered in a more nuanced way. Because he was without sin, Jesus did not personally need to have justifying faith. But if one argues that the *kenosis* means that Jesus had limited knowledge, not only about the world about him, but also about his own future, then it becomes likely that he needed trusting faith. For example, it could be argued, that although Jesus himself did not need saving faith, he did need to trust that his life, death and resurrection, would have a saving and justifying effect on all those who believed in him. As we have seen in the preceding chapters, trusting faith of an intense and certain kind, which is evoked by an experiential conviction about the Father's loving nature and will, is a prerequisite for the performance of deeds of power. As was noted above, the evangelists, especially John, believed that Jesus had received such inspired knowledge from the Father, and relied upon the Spirit at work within him, not only to proclaim the advent of the kingdom, but also to demonstrate its coming in deeds of power. If this understanding of his ministry is correct, then Jesus would have exercised the charism of trusting faith, time and time again. That being so, it could be said that he possessed an 'archetypal faith.' As Avery Dulles has written: 'Even though Jesus, as the incarnate Son, did not have faith in the same sense that other beings do, he exemplifies in an eminent manner the obedience and trust that are constitutive of faith.'[36]

Conclusion

This chapter has been written within a *kenotic* framework. It has stressed the fact that although, as God's divine Son, Jesus was entitled to the beatific vision, he surrendered this right, and became human like us in every way, except for sin. The study of the non-synoptic texts established the fact, that there is reason for saying that not only is Jesus the object of faith, he himself seems to be *the* exemplar *par excellence* of trusting faith. The examination of the synoptic texts indicated that Jesus was in all probability a man who trusted whole-heartedly in his Father. Surely he gave expression to that trust in a particularly poignant way during passion week.

Finally, many Catholics and Protestants have tended to deny that Jesus had faith because of an exegesis, which was more influenced by a theological presupposition, to do with the prerogatives of Christ's divinity, than by the literal meaning of the text. But when the humanity, and therefore, the limitations of Christ's humanity are stressed in the light of a *kenotic* perspective, it is possible to argue that Jesus was indeed a man of remarkable faith. While he didn't need saving faith for himself, he did need to believe that his baptism in suffering, (cf. Mk 10:38) would bring salvation to sinners who believed in him. There is also convincing evidence to indicate that in his ministry Jesus exercised the intense and certain trust, characteristic of the charism of faith, as defined in chapter three. He expressed this faith in his teaching on faith and by performing deeds of power.

Implicit in all of this is the notion that the true disciple not only imitates the faith of Jesus, but through graced union with him, participates in his expectant faith. As the *Catechism of the Catholic Church* says in a striking way in paragraph 521: 'Christ enables us *to live in him* all that he himself lived, and *he lives it in us.*' If this understanding is correct it means that whereas inspired wisdom and knowledge are an aspect of the illuminative stage of the Christian life, inspired trust is an aspect of the unitive stage. Jesus expresses this mystical notion when he says: 'I am the vine, you are the branches. The one who abides in me, and I in him, he it is that bears much fruit, for apart from me you can do nothing' Jn 15:5. One could express this notion in the following Pauline way. I have been crucified with Christ; it is no longer I who live, but Christ who lives in me and exercises the charism of faith and its associated gifts in and through me (cf. Gal 2:20).

CHAPTER FIVE

Jesus on Trust in Providence and Petitionary Prayer

In the previous chapter it was noted how Christologies which stress the humanity of Jesus, tend to believe that he was not only faithful, but pre-eminent in his trust in God and that he probably exercised the charism of faith when he performed deeds of power. The aim of this chapter is to examine the teaching of Jesus about two forms of trusting faith, namely, trust in divine providence and trust in petitionary prayer. It will be augmented by the reflections of Sts James and John on these subjects, in the belief that they constitute an inspired understanding and application of the teaching of the Master. Besides trying to understand what Jesus, James and John had to say about trusting faith, this chapter will try to establish whether they had something like the charism of faith in mind.

Trusting in the Providence of God

Joachim Jeremias has pointed to the fact that trusting faith was of central importance in Christ's teaching: 'In content Jesus' whole message is ... a call to faith, even if the word does not occur very often.'[1] In the synoptic gospels, Jesus does not talk about faith in God's existence, or the fact that there is only one God. Like his Old Testament predecessors he took truths like these for granted. As James reminds us, even the devil believes in such things (cf. Jm 2:19). Jesus does not mention justifying faith either. Rather he talks in typically Jewish fashion about the exercise of trust in the concrete circumstances of everyday life. Wallis and Dufour make the point that if faith is a matter of the *fides quae* and the *fides qua*, Jesus tended to emphasise the subjective disposition of trust as well as the objective faithfulness of God. This was particularly evident in his frequent use of the word *amen*. The Aramaic version was derived from the Hebrew, and literally means: 'Because God is faithful and true to his promises, you can be sure and certain of what I am about to say.'[2]

In a world that he knew to be dangerous and uncertain, Jesus highlighted a number of important points. He declared: 'Blessed are the poor' Lk 6:20 and 'How blessed are the poor in spirit' Mt 5:3. In other words, blessed are those who in their vulnerability and weakness are aware of their desperate need for God. The great Protestant theologian Friedrich Schleiermacher echoed this sentiment when he said that religion was fundamentally the 'feeling of absolute dependence.'[3] People experience the pinch of radical need in a number of characteristic ways. At a fundamental level, there is the sting of contingency. It is based on the awareness that nothing that exists, including, myself, is the adequate explanation of its own existence. All created being is, therefore, threatened by non-being. Admittedly, most people are not consciously aware of this kind of ontological anxiety but it can be indirectly experienced in the following ways. Firstly, there is the problem of material poverty. Poor people, especially in the third world, live on the margins of existence. In their powerlessness they have to depend on such things as the vagaries of the weather, governmental agencies and the generosity of others. Secondly, in the developed world the new poor suffer from, what Mother Teresa referred to as the famine of the heart due to a lack of love. It is often experienced in the form of loneliness, stress, depression, neuroses, addictions and obsessions of different kinds.

As a result of the Abba experience, Jesus' had a powerful intuition of the greatness, goodness and love of God his Father. As Albert Nolan has said: 'We know that the Abba-experience was an experience of God as a compassionate Father. This would mean that Jesus experienced the mysterious creative power behind all phenomena as compassion or love'.[4] He believed that the Holy One cares for the birds of the air, the lilies of the field and in a special way for human beings.

Jesus believed that God in his providence has a benevolent plan for each of our lives. He agreed with Jeremiah who said: 'For surely I know the plans I have for you, says the Lord, plans for your welfare and not for harm, to give you a future and a hope.' Jer 29:11. That plan is expressed in two interrelated ways. Firstly there is our vocation in life whether married or single. Secondly, within the context of our vocation we are guided by the Spirit on a day to day basis. As Cardinal Newman wrote: 'Lead kindly light amid the encircling gloom … I do not ask to see the distant scene, one step enough for me.'

Jesus taught that besides having a plan for our lives, God provides for us in our needs. God's provision is experienced in two ways, firstly internally in the form of graces. As Paul says in Phil 2:13, 'It is God who is at work in you, enabling you both to will and to work for his good pleasure.' Secondly, God's provision is experienced in external ways in the form of material benefits. As Jesus said: 'You must not set your hearts on things to eat and things to drink; nor must you worry. It is the gentiles of this world who set their hearts on all these things. Your Father well knows you need them. No set your hearts on his kingdom, and these other things will be given you as well' Lk 12:30.

Jesus believed that God's providence embraces evil and transforms it, much as the oyster transforms the irritating presence of grit within itself, into a beautiful pearl. No matter what weaknesses people have, what mistakes they make, or what sins they commit, they are integrated into God's plan and embraced by his providence. As a result they can become the birthplace of blessing. Evil doesn't have the last word, that word belongs to God, and it is a word of blessing and victory. That was evident when Jesus prayed that Peter would be comforted by the Holy Spirit following his cowardly denial of his master. (cf. Lk 22:31-32). St Paul grasped the nature of this paradoxical dynamic when he said: 'where sin abounds the grace of God more abounds' Rom 5:20.

Trusting in the power of Petitionary Prayer

The First Vatican Council described divine providence as follows: 'God protects and governs by his providence all things he has made, "reaching from end to end mightily, and ordering all things well" For "all things are bare and open to his eyes" even those which are yet to come into existence by the free action of creatures.'[5] The pre-eminent way of expressing trust in divine providence is to have firm confidence in the power of petitionary prayer. Jesus' teaching on this subject is informed by his vivid awareness of the goodness and faithfulness of God the Father. The importance of this point cannot be overemphasised. Those who, through the Spirit's help, enjoy the Abba experience (cf. Rom 8:15; Gal 4:6), know that the Lord wants what is best for us. This powerful intuition is expressed in a number of texts. In Lk 15:31 the Prodigal Father says: 'You are with me always, *all I have is yours*.' In Mt 7:11, Jesus says: 'If you parents, who are evil, know how to give good gifts to your children, *how much more will your Father who is in heaven give good things to those who ask him*.' Later St Paul echoed these sentiments in Rom 8:32 when he observed: 'If God has given us his Son *would he not give us all things in him*.' In other words, it is only by a childlike, humble, and heartfelt trust in the loving dependability of God (cf. Mt 11:25; Lk 10:21), that we can experience the generosity of the Father. Evidently the Lord is God-with-us, the benevolent One who will give us whatever we ask.

At this point, we will explore the way in which Jesus looked for faith either in those who petitioned him for help, or in their relatives and friends. As Perrin points out, unlike Hellenistic or Rabbinic healers,[6] Jesus needed a response of faith from the people who sought his assistance. When he restored the sight of two blind men who asked for his help, he touched their eyes and said, 'Let it be done for you according to your faith' Mt 9:29. When the father of the epileptic boy asked him for assistance, Jesus declared that: 'all things can be done for the one who believes,' to which the distraught man replied, 'I believe; help my unbelief' Mk 9:23-24. By way of contrast we are told that when Jesus went to visit his neighbours in Nazareth, by and large, he was unable to respond to their requests for help 'because of their unbelief' Mt 13:58.

In other places, in the gospels, the faith of a relative or friend was important. This is clear in the healing of the court official's son in Jn 4:47-53. We are told that 'the man believed the word that Jesus spoke to him', and even before he got home his servants told him that his son had recovered. In the story of the cure of the centurion's servant in Mt 8:5-13, Jesus said: 'Truly, I tell you, in no one in Israel have I found such faith,' and a little later, 'Go back, then; let this be done for you, as your faith demands.' We are informed that his servant was healed at that very hour. There was also the case of the paralysed man who was lowered through the roof by his faith-full friends in Mk 2:3-11. The anointed one responded to their trust, and as the evangelist says, 'when he saw their faith, Jesus said to the man, "My son your sins are forgiven",' and later, 'I say to you, stand up, take your bed and go home.'

A question we can ask at this point is this, what measure of faith was displayed by those who asked Jesus to bless them? Was it wishful faith of the hesitant kind, or expectant faith of the unhesitating kind? Before answering these questions, a number of observations. Trusting, confident faith relies on the goodness and providence of God in the expectation that a prayer request is being answered already, or will soon be answered by the Lord, in accord with the divine promises and love. As Jesus declared: 'Whatever you ask for in prayer, *believing you have received it,* will be yours' Mk 11:24. In the Greek the aorist is used in an anticipatory way. In other words, the person praying believes that what he or she is asking for has begun to be granted in the here and now. Implicit in this use of the 'prophetic present,' is the notion that in spite of all evidence to the contrary, the seed of future blessing has already been planted in the soil of the present. In time they will take root and bear fruit in a visible way. Instead of praying with the *hope* that God *may* answer the prayer *if* it is offered in accord with the divine will, (i.e. praying with belief and hope) it is offered in the confident *expectation* that that God *is* answering the prayer, because it is known – as a result of inspired knowledge – that the prayer is in accord with the divine will (i.e. praying with expectant faith).

It seems clear enough, that the experiential awareness of God's will, and the consequent sense of inner certainty, is a special grace, which isn't necessarily granted in every situation. Many people know this to be true from their own experience of the Christian life. There is an important question to be kept in mind at this point: is expectant faith of the unhesitating kind synonymous with the charism of faith, or are they actually different?

An Archetypal Example

Instead of answering these questions in a general way, or examining many texts, we will focus on Mk 5:24-34 which was mentioned in chapter two. It describes the cure the haemorrhaging woman. Mann says in his commentary on Mark, that whereas Matthew's version of this incident is basically a miracle story, in Mark it is essentially a text about faith. Marshall says much the same.[7]

> Now there was a woman who had suffered from a hemorrhage for twelve years; after long and painful treatment under various doctors, she had spent all she had without being any better for it; in fact she was getting worse. She had heard about Jesus, and she came up through the crowd and touched his cloak from behind, thinking, 'If I can touch his clothes, I shall be saved.' And at once the source of the bleeding dried up, and she felt in herself that she was cured of her complaint. And at once aware of the power that had gone out from him, Jesus turned round in the crowd and said, 'Who touched my clothes?' His disciples said to him. 'You see the crowd is pressing round you; how can you ask, "who touched me?"' But he continued to look all round to see who had done it. Then the woman came forward, frightened and trembling because she knew what had happened to her and she fell at his feet and told him the whole truth. 'My daughter,' he said, 'your faith has restored you to health; go in peace and be free of your complaint.'

In this story faith has an archetypal quality. If the charism of faith is operative in this healing, it is likely that it is also operative in other healing accounts as well. In chapter two, it was noted how St Paul thought that there were four interconnected elements in the experience of salvation by means of justifying faith. Analogously, there are four similar steps in the experience of healing by means of expectant faith.

Acknowledgment of Need

Firstly, there is the acknowledgment of need. The haemorrhaging woman was one of the poor in spirit. She was not only suffering from a chronic menstrual problem, she also had to cope with its social and religious consequences. No wonder her condition is referred to as 'a scourge' or 'whip.' It may suggest that her affliction was regarded as a punishment for sin. As far as the Jewish religion was concerned, she was ritually unclean (cf. Lev 15:19) and therefore excluded from the community and its worship, because it was thought that her impurity was communicable by touch. It also meant that she would be unable to marry, and if she was already married she would be unable to bear children. We are told that she had searched in vain for a medical cure. The poor woman was painfully and even desperately aware of her urgent need for physical healing, and through it, for re-integration with the civil and religious community. What is exceptional in this story is the fact that she did not make her need known to Jesus. Instead she reached out anonymously to touch the hem of his garment from behind. It has been suggested by some commentators, that this act betrayed a magical mentality. But it is more likely that as someone who was ritually unclean, she did not want to make Jesus unclean by touching him, or by talking to him in public. Hers was a sensitive prayer in action.

Hearing the Good News

Secondly, she needed to hear the good news. Presumably, she had not only heard about Jesus, she had observed him closely and listened to him preaching. His presence seems to have made a deep impression on her and his message seems to have found a place in her heart. Taken together they led to a rudimentary form of *gnosis* or inspired knowledge. Jesus was a man of God, a compassionate instrument of divine power.

Responding with Faith

Thirdly, there is a need for faith. The woman's awareness of Jesus and his word had evoked a faith that went beyond magical thinking. Was it faith of the wishful hesitating kind, or faith of the expectant unhesitating kind? The answer is clear in the text. Instead of saying: 'If I touch even his clothes, I *may* be healed, *if* it is God's will,' she says, 'If I touch even his clothes, I *shall* be healed.' Her inner sense of confidence is an example of what Jesus had in mind when he said: 'I tell you, whatever you ask for in prayer, believe that you *have* received it and it will be yours' Mk 11:24. The fact that her desire was in accordance with God's will, and that she had expectant faith, was confirmed by events. As soon as the woman, touched Jesus' garment, '*she knew in herself* that she was cured of her affliction' Mk 5:29.

Confession of Faith

Fourthly, the woman confesses her faith. When Jesus realised that power had gone out from him, he wanted to know who had touched him. Knowing that she was the one, the woman spoke up. Instead of causing her to be afraid, the woman's awareness of having been healed, was the reason she courageously overcome her feelings of timidity and revealed herself to Jesus. This is another aspect of her healing, Her public confession not only sealed her physical healing, it overcame her civil and religious alienation. Jesus commended her for her trust, and confirmed her healing, when he said, 'Daughter, your faith has saved you. Go in peace and be healed of your scourge.' The address, of 'daughter' is warm and confirms the woman's socio-religious healing and reintegration with the community. He acknowledges that her unhesitating faith was the key to her healing. The word for healing in verses 23, 28 and 34 is derived from *sozo.* In Greek, it has two related meanings, 'to save' and 'to heal.'[8] Both are encapsulated in the final words of Jesus, 'go in *peace,* and be healed of your scourge.' As Dufour has pointed out, the words for peace, *shalom* in Hebrew, and *eirene* in Greek, when taken together, mean, wholeness, integrity, and the tranquil possession of good things and above all health.[9] But at a deeper level, this story is symbolic of the healing that would come through faith in the saving death and resurrection of Jesus.

Back to the all important question. Is the expectant faith exercised by the woman in this account, synonymous with the charism of faith? In terms of the analytical definition in chapter three, it would seem that it fails to satisfy criterion five, namely, that the charism of faith should *express* itself in a deed of power. In this case, it is Jesus rather than the woman who is the source of the healing. But all healing is ultimately from God whether the person is the channel (cf. 1 Cor 12:9) or the recipient (cf. Mk 5:29). So the words 'mainly manifested' in criterion five should be understood to refer either to the commission, or to the reception of a deed of power. If this is so, then expectant faith, involving super-eminent certainty, amounts to the charism of faith if it leads to the experience of a deed of power such as a healing or for that matter some other impressive answer to prayer such as the conversion of a sinner. This conclusion would also apply to cases where the expectant faith of friends or neighbours leads to events such as the healing or exorcism of someone else.

Prerequisites for Answered Prayer

Exegetes point to the fact that most of Jesus' teaching about prayer has to do with its petitionary form. Rooted in the notion of creaturely dependence on God, and expressed in a series of remarkable promises, it encourages those who pray, to have complete confidence in God. The Lord undertakes to answer our prayers, but like all biblical promises they can only be fulfilled if certain conditions are met. There are a number of them mentioned in the gospels. Not surprisingly there is a certain amount of overlap, and one or two of them may already have been adverted to. They are listed here without exegitical commentary.

Petitions are made in the name of Jesus, e.g. Jn 16:23 says: 'In that day you will no longer ask me anything. I tell you the truth, my Father will give you whatever you ask in my name. Until now you have not asked for anything in my name. Ask and you will receive, and your joy will be complete.'

Petitions will be granted if we abide in Christ and hear his word, e.g. Jn 15:7 says: 'If you remain in me and my words remain in you, ask whatever you wish, and it will be given you.'

The petitioner must pray with a heart free from resentment, e.g. Mk 11:25 says: 'And when you stand praying, if you hold anything against anyone, forgive him.'

If possible prayer should have a community dimension and be offered in union with others, e.g. Mt 18:19 says: 'Again, I tell you that if two of you on earth agree about anything you ask for, it will be done for you by my Father in heaven.'

Petitions should be in conformity with God's will as ex-

pressed in the Lord's Prayer, e.g. Mt 6:10 says: 'Your kingdom come, your will be done on earth as it is in heaven.'
As the parable of the Pharisee and the Publican makes clear, Jesus believed that the petition which is offered in a humble rather than a self-righteous spirit will be heard Lk 18:9-14.
Petitions need to be offered with perseverance, e.g. echoing the parables of the friend at midnight, and the widow and the unjust judge, Mt 7:7-8 says: 'Ask and it will be given to you; seek and you will find; knock and the door will be opened to you. For everyone who asks receives; he who seeks finds; and to him who knocks, the door will be opened.'
Prayers need to be offered in a spirit of expectant faith, e.g. Mark 11:24 says: 'Therefore I tell you, whatever you ask for in prayer, believe that you have received it, and it will be yours.'

St James on the Power of Petitionary Prayer

Although it could have been written by a pseudonymous author around or after 100 A.D.[10] it seems likely that James – who may have been related to Jesus, and also leader of the church in Jerusalem – wrote the letter before his death about 62 A.D. He says this about petitionary prayer:

> If any of you is lacking in wisdom, ask God, who gives to all generously and ungrudgingly, and it will be given you. But ask in faith, never doubting, for the one who doubts, is like a wave of the sea, driven and tossed by the wind; for the doubter, being double-minded and unstable in every way, must not expect to receive anything from the Lord. Jm 1:5-6.

At the beginning of his letter, James points to the fact that the Christian community needs faith in order to persevere during times of sickness, poverty and persecution. He then goes on to say that if people lack anything, such as wisdom, they should ask God for it. Rather than being theoretical in nature, the wisdom James has in mind, concerns the practical insight necessary to discover God's will and lead a good life. His perspective was rooted in the wisdom literature of the Old Testament and he referred to it again in 3:13; 17f. In advocating this kind of awareness he was opposing an elitist and divisive sort of wisdom which was being advocated by some of the Jerusalem Church. Indeed he referred to it as 'earthly, human and devilish' 3:15.

James goes on to say that if the disciples want such wisdom, they have to engage in petitionary prayer and ask for it. Two points can be made about this. Firstly, the phrase 'ask God for wisdom,' is rooted in the Old Testament. In Wis 7:7 we read: 'And so I prayed, and understanding was given me; I entreated and the spirit of Wisdom came to me.' Secondly, the phrase 'ask God' finds an echo in the gospels. In this connection commentators refer to many of the sayings of Jesus such as Mt 7:7;11; Lk 1:9; Jn 16:23; Mt 21:21-22; and Mk 11:23-24. James says that prayer can be made with expectant faith for two reasons. Firstly, God is generous to all. Everyone, who prays can be confident that the Father is equally interested in his or her particular prayers. As Johnson observes, 'the giving of God ... is universal, unequivocal and generous.'[11] Secondly, James says that God 'neither grudges or reproaches anyone.' In other words, confidence in prayer need not be compromised by an awareness of unworthiness. The Lord doesn't hold our sins against us in a scolding or reproachful way. This point is adverted to in *The Shepherd of Hermas*. In 9.1, the author states that the believer should not say: 'How can I ask anything from the Lord and receive it after having sinned so greatly against him?' It is this twofold awareness, that enables a person to pray with complete assurance.

James then proceeds to say – and it is the crucial verse, 'prayer must be made with faith, and no trace of doubt.' What kind of faith has the apostle in mind here? Is it trusting faith of the hesitant kind or expectant faith of an unhesitating, charismatic kind? Mention of prayer which is offered without doubt in the heart is reminiscent of the words of Jesus in Mk 11:23 and Mt 21:21, where he says that believers will be able to exercise mountain-moving authority if they have no hesitation in their hearts. Although none of the commentators advert to this point, James seems to see a certain parallel between the generosity of God who gives to all in an unreserved way, and the faith of the believer who should give unreserved trust to the Lord. Dibelius makes two very interesting observations in this regard. Firstly, he says that Jesus required this kind of faith in the Synoptic miracle stories and cites many examples.[12] Secondly, he says the kind of faith James is referring to is equivalent to the charism of faith mentioned by St Paul in 1 Cor 12:9; 13:2. He writes: 'And as inappropriate as it would be to drag in here what Paul otherwise calls faith, nevertheless the "faith" which he mentions among the "gifts of the Spirit" *is certainly this faith* that a request will be granted, that the miracle will happen' (1 Cor 12:9; 13:2; 2 Cor 8:7; Gal 5:22).[13]

James observes, that prayer is not always offered with certainty in the heart. The desire and trust of some people is weakened by doubt. Such double minded men and women are like unstable waves on the sea, which are blown here and there by the wind. They have no reason, says James, to expect anything from their prayers. Surely, what is implicit in this verse is the distinction, already made, between trust of the wishful, hesitating kind, and trust of the expectant, unhesitating kind. It is the gift of wisdom, which enables God's word of promise to change from being a notional truth that commands the assent of the mind about what God *could* do in the *future,* into a revelatory word of wisdom which commands the assent of the heart about what God *is* beginning to do in the *present*. When James referred to the wave on the sea blown by the wind, perhaps he had the double mindedness of St Peter in mind. He began to walk with certain faith on the water, and then sank beneath its surface as soon as doubt entered his heart. While it is probably impossible to prove whether James had that example in view, it is a relevant one nevertheless. It is only when people can pray with expectant faith, characterised by heartfelt certainty, that they can expect God to act in a powerful way in response to their petitions. Surely, our own everyday experience endorses the truth of James' teaching.

Later in his letter St James has this further comment to make about petitionary prayer:

> The heartfelt prayer of someone upright works very powerfully. Elijah was a human being as frail as ourselves – he prayed earnestly for it not to rain, and no rain fell for

three and a half years; then he prayed again and the sky gave rain and the earth gave crops. Jm 5:16-19.

These verses are connected thematically with the ones we have just examined. James illustrates what he means by prayer offered with undoubting faith, by citing the example of the prophet Elijah. He stresses the fact that heartfelt prayer, like his, is necessary. In the Old Testament the Lord promised to respond to earnest prayer of this kind e.g. in Deut 4:29 and Jer 29:12-15. James's reference to the 'righteous' is not intended to be loaded with dogmatic implications. It simply means that the prayer of people who are devout in the traditional Jewish sense, is efficacious. This belief can be traced back to the Old Testament, e.g. Ps 33:16,18; Prov 15:29 and Sir 35:16-18 which states: 'Whoever wholeheartedly serves God will be accepted, his petitions will carry to the clouds. The prayer of the humble pierces the clouds: and until it does, he is not to be consoled, nor will he desist until the Most High takes notice of him.'

Elijah was such a man. Although, in Jewish eyes he was a superstar of faith, James is at pains to point out that in reality he was a mere mortal like the rest of us, a man with human frailties who knew how to pray from the heart with expectant faith. So Elijah is not just a saint to be admired, he is also an ordinary human being to be imitated. As Sir 48:1-11 indicates, he was revered as a man of prayer. James goes on to cite an example of his powers of intercession. In 1 Kings 17:1 we read that the prophet foretold a drought: 'By the life of Yahweh, God of Israel, whom I serve, there will be neither dew nor rain these coming years unless I give the word.'

It is interesting to note that there is no explicit reference to prayer in this verse. Johnson suggests, however, that it may be implicit in the phrase 'by the life of Yahweh' which may be an oath type prayer.[14] But there was a traditional understanding that it was as a result of intercessory prayer that Elijah had closed the heavens. As Rev 11:6 says speaking of people of prayer: 'They have the power to lock up the sky so that it does not rain as long as they are prophesying.' James' view that it did not rain for three and a half years was deduced from a rabbinical tradition perhaps, and from 1 Kings 18:1 which say: 'A long time went by, and the word of Yahweh came to Elijah in the third year, "Go present yourself to Ahab, and I will send rain on the country".' After Elijah prayed we are told that a cloud from the sea appeared and 'there was a great rain' (1 Kings 18:44).

St John on Petitionary Prayer

The focus of attention shifts, now, to the first letter of John. Raymond Brown comes to the conclusion that this epistle was written after the gospel of John, i.e. post 90 A.D. and by a different author from the same Johannine community.[15] The epistle was authored within a context of Christian conflict. From a dogmatic point of view, some schismatic members of the community were Gnostic Docetists who denied Christ's true humanity. From a moral point of view they adhered to perfectionistic and dualistic values, e.g. that true freedom and holiness are achieved not by baptism but by freeing one's soul from worldly attachments. 1 Jn 5:14-16 is written with this background in mind. It is about the power of petitionary prayer, specifically, prayer for errant members of the believing community. Firstly, the author says:

> And this is the confidence we have in him, that if we ask anything according to his will, he hears us. And if we know that he hears us in whatever we ask, we know that we have obtained the requests made of him.

Confidence in God involves three related points. Firstly, there is a general confidence in one's salvation and the prospect of eternal redemption. Secondly, this form of confidence acts as a backdrop for a sense of conviction about the efficacy of petitionary prayer, offered by the community in the particular circumstances of everyday life. Thirdly, its sense of certainty is informed more often than not, by the promises of scripture, especially those to do with God's willingness to answer prayer.

John says that it is important to pray in accord with the will of God. Two points are involved here. Firstly, from a Johannine point of view, those who want their prayers to be granted, need to live, as best they can, in accord with the commandments as encapsulated in the great command of love (cf. 1 Jn 3:23). Secondly, prayer should not be selfish or arbitrary, but led by the Spirit and in accord with God's will (cf. Gal 5:16; Mt 6:10).

Although John doesn't mention them, there is no reason to exclude the gifts of wisdom and knowledge and their ability to reveal what God wants. As John says elsewhere: 'The anointing which you received from him abides in you, and you have no need that anyone should teach you; as his anointing teaches you about everything' 1 Jn 2:27. It is this anointing of the Holy Spirit which helps people to discover the will of God in the circumstances of daily life, – in this particular case as we shall see – how to deal with someone who has fallen into public sin.

We know, John declares, that if people pray in this way, not only are they heard, they have *already obtained* what they asked for. This awareness displays a remarkable degree of expectant faith, one shot-through with super-eminent certainty characteristic of the charism of faith. In terms of what Jesus said in Mk 11:24, it believes that it *has already received* what was asked for in faith. Once again, *present certainty* is the basis of *future hope*, faith conviction in the here and now, a sure pledge of blessings to come. It seems clear that in these verses John is going beyond trusting faith of the conditional kind, to the charism of faith of the expectant kind.

Just as James illustrated the power of petitionary prayer by citing the example of Elijah, so now, John illustrates its potential efficacy by saying it can bring about repentance in the lives of sinners. He writes in 1 Jn 5:16, 'If you see your brother or sister committing what is not a mortal sin, you will ask and God will give life to such a one – to those whose sin is not mortal.' Raymond Brown has pointed out that scripture scholars have many differing interpretations of the difficult phrase 'a sin not unto death.'[16] The reference, here, to mortal sin, is not to 'ordinary' grave sins but to some extremely deadly sin such as the sin against the Holy Spirit or apostasy. Bruce Vawter says that the author of the epistle does not mean: 'Simply mortal sin as distinguished from venial sin, for the "sins unto death" in this context also include mortal sins. It is possible that he has in mind the activity of the "Antichrists" previously mentioned (2:18-29).'[17]

Pheme Perkins, concurs. She says that John has Mt 18:15-20 in mind. It is a passage that describes the three point procedure involved in trying to convert an errant brother or sister from his or her sinful ways.[18] However, if the sin alienates the person from the Christian community there is no point in praying for him or her. She argues that when the Johannine author speaks here about petitionary prayer, he hasn't petitions in general in mind, but rather prayer for a non-schismatic member of the community who has fallen into some kind of public sin, e.g. robbery or sexual promiscuity. If the community, pray with the kind of expectant faith already mentioned, 1 John 5:16 promises that the prodigal will eventually come to his or her senses, and will repent.

Does the kind of petitionary prayer, mentioned by the author of 1 Jn 5:14-16, involve charismatic faith? A careful examination of the text indicates that the criteria mentioned in the definition of the charism of faith seem to be satisfied. Prayer goes beyond trusting faith of the wishful hesitant kind, to become an inspired form of expectant faith, graced by a serene inner certainty that God will respond sooner or later, by manifesting his power and granting the grace of true repentance. St Monica's effective prayer for the conversion of Augustine is an outstanding example of the Johannine teaching in action. Although it had a specific form of petitionary prayer in mind, there seems to be no real reason why it couldn't be extended to apply to any kind of need.

Conclusion

In a well known conference on prayer Abbot John Cassian (c. 360-435 A.D.) said that many of the Church Fathers in the East, believed that the spirituality of the entire bible could be encapsulated in the phrase, 'O God come to my assistance, O Lord make haste to help me' Ps 70:1.[19] It seems to express two fundamental and interrelated aspects of the teaching of Jesus. Firstly, we should have absolute trust in the providence of God. Secondly, we should express that trust in all our moments of need, whether material or spiritual, by making our requests to God. It is clear that like Jesus, James and John taught that petitionary prayer of this kind will be efficacious when it offered to God with expectant faith of an unhesitating kind. There is also good reason to think that this kind of trust can, at times, have the characteristics of the charism of faith mentioned by St Paul in 1 Cor 12:9.

CHAPTER SIX

Jesus on Firm Faith and the Prayer of Command

Absolute dependence on the providence of God can find expression in the prayer of petition. As we have seen, a person can pray in the hope that God may do something in the future, if what is asked is in accordance with God's will, e.g. 'Lord I know that nothing is impossible to you. I ask you, if it is your will, to heal this person whom you love.' A person with expectant or charismatic faith accepts that the promises of God are true at a notional level. But as a result of a divine inspiration, in a particular situation of need, he or she has no inner doubt about them and confidently believes that God is acting, or soon will act, in the here and now. Sometimes such a person will be led to pray a prayer of *command,* e.g. 'Lord, nothing is impossible to you. In your Name I say to this sickness, yield to the healing power of God at work within you, and I thank you Lord, that even now your Spirit is hastening to fulfil your loving will.' The future hope of a prayer of command like this, is rooted in present conviction. As the letter to the Hebrews 11:1 puts it: 'Faith is the assurance (in the present) of things hoped for (in the future), the conviction (in the present) of things not seen (in the future).'

Jesus spoke on a number of occasions about the relationship between faith filled prayers of command and deeds of power. To understand his teaching, we begin with, four texts which refer to moving metaphorical mountains and trees of difficulty (i.e. Mk 11:12-24; Mt 21:18-22; and Mt 17:19-20; Lk 17:5-6). We will seek to establish whether they refer to the charism of faith or not. There are a number of reasons for choosing these passages in particular. Firstly, mention of mountain moving faith, in the synoptic gospels, is reminiscent of Paul's phrase, 'if I have faith to move mountains,' in 1 Cor 13:2, and therefore by association with the charism of faith in 1 Cor 12:9. Secondly, scripture scholars believe that these texts are particularly significant, because they seem to refer, in one way or another, to a remarkably firm form of trusting faith.[1] Following the analysis of these texts, a number of related ones will be examined to establish whether they refer to the charism of faith or not.

Faith to move Mountains

The evangelists situate the texts to do with moving mountains or trees on the road from Bethany to Jerusalem, during the last week of Christ's life. On the way, Jesus cursed a fig tree for not bearing fruit, and the next day, Peter noticed that it had withered and died from the roots upwards. He said to Jesus:

> 'Rabbi, look! The fig tree that you cursed has withered.' Jesus answered them, 'Have faith in God (or if you have faith). Truly I tell you, if you say to this mountain, 'Be taken up and thrown into the sea,' and if you do not doubt in your heart, but believe that what you say will come to pass, it will be done for you. So I tell you , whatever you ask for in prayer, believe that you have received it (are receiving) and it will be yours.'

The parallel passage in Matthew's Gospel concludes with the words, 'Whatever you ask in prayer with faith, you will receive.'

The extended quotation from Mark is situated within a complex chapter which contains five interconnected episodes;

Mk 11: 1-11, the entry into Jerusalem
Mk 11:12-14, the cursing of the fig tree
Mk 11:15-19, the cleansing of the temple
Mk 11:20-25, the discovery that the fig tree has withered, and Jesus' teaching on faith, prayer and mutual forgiveness
Mk 11:27-33, the challenge to Jesus' authority

Meier, looks at the chapter within its literary and theological context. He suggests that originally, the pre-Marcan source for this chapter included three elements; Jesus' entry into Jerusalem; his cleansing of the temple; and the challenge to his authority. As this tradition developed, the pre-Marcan author, upon whom the evangelist relied, emphasised that the cleansing of the temple was not an act of purification and reform, but rather a prophetic judgment on the temple, and the unrepentant temple community. He did this by inventing the story of the cursing of the fig tree. It is a difficult one to interpret. Mann says: 'Either Jesus thought that in him the New Age was dawning and that, therefore, the fig tree should already be showing signs of that age, or the fig tree was itself a demonstration of the fact that the New Age was not yet ready to be ushered in ... The notion of the tree withering to its roots is reminiscent of a similar account in Jonah 4:7. It shows that the word Jesus spoke, had the power to accomplish what it said, i.e. the death of the tree.' Meier adds in similar vein: 'Mk 11:22-24 apparently makes Jesus' powerful curse of the fig tree *a paradigm of the power of faith filled prayer*, despite the fact that this curse miracle, like most of the miracle stories in Mark, says nothing about Jesus praying or believing.'[2] In any case, just as the fruitless tree was cursed, so the temple and its cult would die only to be replaced by the new community of faith. Mark who adopted this pre-existing material, and added a theological dimension by tacking on pre-existing sayings about faith, prayer and forgiveness. They now take centre stage as the focus of our attention.

Jesus responds to Peter's cry of amazement on seeing the withered, fig tree by saying, 'Have faith in God.' Apparently, the Greek phrase is unique, and is hardly defensible from a grammatical point of view. It has been translated in a number of ways. Some later manuscripts, render the phrase as, 'if you have faith in God.' Other translations opt for, 'whoever believes,' or 'you have God's faithfulness,' i.e. you hold on to God with the faithfulness he displays towards you. Derek Prince and George Montague maintain that what Jesus actually said in its most literal form, was, 'have God's faith,' in others words, through the gift of the Spirit, share in God's own faith.[3] However one translates the Greek phrase, it seems clear that it does not refer either to justifying faith or to the fruit of the Spirit. This would imply that Jesus was referring solely to unwavering trust in the Lord and firm confidence in our ability to share in God's powerful activity. The injunction has an eschatological dimension in so far as words and deeds of power inaugurate the New Age.

Incidentally, this latter point satisfies criterion six of the definition of the charism of faith in chapter three.

The verse in Mk 11:23, about commanding a mountain to move into the sea, is a key one, because it is similar to 1 Cor 13:2, where the moving of mountains requires the exercise of the charism of faith. Jesus introduces his point by saying, 'Truly I say to you.' This phrase has already occurred in Mk 3:28. As was noted in chapter two, it is rooted in the Hebrew *'mn* meaning, 'to show oneself firm and stable.' So the words 'truly I say to you,' can be paraphrased to read, 'you can really trust in what I'm about to say to you because it is a divinely attested fact.' Incidentally, Marshall points out, that this promise is addressed not only to the apostles but to all who believe in their teaching.[4]

Scripture scholars seem to be agreed that references to moving mountains and uprooting trees were proverbial sayings in the New Testament era, and referred to making possible what seemed impossible.[5] There are at least three mountains that Jesus may have had in mind, either the Mount of Olives, Mount Zion or Mount Gerazim. In the light of his polemic against the temple, it is possible that he was referring to Zion the temple mount. However, the Dead Sea is more likely. It would have just about been visible from the Mount of Olives on a clear day. Normally when Jesus talked about faith, he did so in terms of the people's need to have faith in order to experience a deed of power. On this occasion however, he talks about the need for faith in order to share in the authority and power of God.

Mk 11:23 says that the disciples who have faith in God will be able to tell a mountain to move, into the sea. It is unlikely that Jesus intended this phrase to be understood in a literal way. As hyperbole, it refers, rather, to everyday obstacles which stand in the path of the coming of the Kingdom of God, such as spiritual oppression and disease. Marshall, points out that the context in which the saying occurs, also indicates that a word of undoubting faith would be sufficient to overcome the 'mountain of unbelief' evident in the religious authorities of his day.[6] The second observation to be made about this verse is the surprising fact that Jesus doesn't encourage those who have faith in God to ask the Father to move the mountain. Instead he encourages them to have such faith in God that they themselves can receive and dispose of the power of the Lord by means of a word of authority. Like all biblical promises this one is associated with certain conditions or 'if' clauses. Jesus says, that the ability to participate in the purposes of God, even to the point of exorcisms, healings and miracles, depends upon the ability of the believers to speak the word of power without any doubt in their hearts.

The word 'heart' in Greek is *kardia.* It referred in a metaphorical way to the seat of feeling and desire, thought and understanding, will and the religious self . In other words, 'heart' referred to the innermost self (cf. Eph 3:16; Rom 8:27; 1 Pt 3:4). It is there that one discerns with certainty that God will act. This kind of inner certainty depends on three things. Firstly, an intimate relationship between God and the believer. Secondly, an experiential, rather than a notional knowledge of God's will. Writing about this important point Marshall observes: 'The exertion of God's transcendent power, which faith seeks, is always subject to the constraint of God's will. The certainty of faith, in other words, presupposes *revelatory insight* into the divine intention, though this must be actualised by the believer's volitional commitment to refuse doubt and seek undivided faith (cf. 5:36; 9:22-24).'[7] Writing about the kind of faith Jesus expected Edward O' Connor observed: 'Evidently, the faith which He is speaking of is not belief in the strict sense of assent to a truth, but the *confident expectation,* based on trust in God, which should animate our prayer. Future events, *without a special revelation about them,* can only be the object of hope and not belief.'[8] Thirdly, one needs a commission to exercise such delegated authority (cf. 3:14; 6:7; 12). Therefore the charism of faith is not the result of wishful thinking, 'psyching' oneself up, or mere mental assent to the promises of God. As Ignatius of Loyola once observed: 'It is not much knowledge that fills and satisfies the soul, but *the intimate understanding and relish of the truth.*'[9] If the person, has such an awareness and firm confidence, God will move the mountain. It is not the believer who performs the deed of power, it is God's power working in and through him or her.

The evangelist adds a final point in Mk 11:25. Un-forgiveness is a block to this kind of gratuitous faith. Authentic Christian prayer, is repentant, a matter of experiencing God's saving mercy, and offering that same mercy to those who have injured and hurt us. To withhold forgiveness, for whatever reason, is to loose the inner witness of God's immediate presence and inspirations, upon which the prayer and word of faith, both depend.

Jesus Talks about Expectant Faith

The following words were spoken by Jesus in response to a question posed by the disciples, when they – unlike Jesus – failed to deliver a boy from an evil spirit.

> Then the disciples came to Jesus privately and said, 'Why could we not cast it out?' He said to them, 'Because of your little faith. For truly I tell you, if you have faith the size of a mustard seed, you will say to this mountain, "Move from here to there," and it will move; and nothing will be impossible for you.'

In Luke's Gospel, the following words occur in a different context and do not follow the story about the possessed boy.

> The apostles said to the Lord, 'Increase our faith!' The Lord replied, 'If you had faith the size of a (grain of) mustard seed, you could say to this mulberry tree, 'Be uprooted and planted in the sea,' and it would obey you.

When the disciples ask why, unlike him, they were unable to cast out the demon, Jesus said it was because of their little faith. In fact Jesus laments two things. Firstly, that the present generation is a faithless one which, like the Jews of old, has failed to believe either in his message or his deeds of power. Secondly, he is disappointed with the disciples, not because they are unbelieving like so many of their contemporaries, but because their faith is the kind, which as Meier points out, '*understands* and assents, but which does not *trust* God totally.'[10] There is the kind of faith whereby I acknowledge something to be true, and the kind whereby I trust a faithful person completely. The assent of the mind should be the expression of the trust of the heart, often it is a substitute for it.

Jesus then goes on to say that if the disciples had real faith, even the size of a mustard seed, they would be able to say to a mountain, 'be moved from here to there' (Mt), or to a mulberry tree, 'be uprooted and cast into the sea' (Lk), and it would happen. What does Jesus mean, when he refers to faith the size of a mustard seed? Apparently, the mustard seed was considered to be the smallest object perceptible to the human eye. But according to Perrin, the point of the image is not that a mustard seed grows into a large bush, but that there is no such thing as a large mustard seed![11] As a result one commentator maintains that 'what counts is faith, not the quantity of faith.'[12] But such a comment does not really explain what the phrase means. After all, Jesus has just regretted the fact that the disciples had 'little faith,' that is precisely the reason why they couldn't respond effectively to the father's request for help. Jesus' saying about the mustard seed, only makes sense if he is referring to a different kind of faith. It goes beyond the assent of the mind, and even the confidence of the heart, to an unheard of certainty about what God is willing to do, in and through the believer. In other words, what Jesus seems to be referring to, is the charism of faith mentioned in the definition, in chapter three. When even a mustard grain of such faith is present 'nothing will be impossible to the believer' Mt 17:20.

Problematic Texts

If this contention is correct it can act as an interpretative key that helps to unlock the meaning of many texts which might otherwise be misinterpreted. Three examples will be examined. There are a number of reasons for doing so. Firstly, it is arguable that they are among those texts which are prone to the misinterpretations already mentioned. Secondly, while these are probably not the only texts in which Jesus seems to talk about the charism of faith, they are the most likely ones.

A) Doing Greater Works than Jesus

In Jn 14:12-14 Jesus says:

> In all truth I tell you, whoever believes in me will perform the same works as I do myself, and will perform even greater works, because I am going to the Father. Whatever you ask in my name I will do, so that the Father may be glorified in the Son. If you ask me anything in my name I will do it.

Taken at face value this promise says, 'If I have proclaimed the coming of the kingdom of God in word, and demonstrated its coming in deeds of power such as exorcisms, healings and miracles, believe me, you will do the same and even greater things, when you receive the Holy Spirit.' Implicit in such an understanding is the presumption that the charism of faith will make possible such deeds of power. But without such an understanding, this passage is hard to interpret. For example, Luther believed that healing and miracles were given to the New Testament Church so that subsequent generations could later do 'greater works than these' by teaching, converting, and saving people spiritually. In one of his sermon's 'On Keeping Children in School,' he talks about the importance of the preaching ministry and goes on to say: 'Is this not an immeasurably greater and more glorious work and miracle than if it were in a bodily or temporal way to raise the dead again to life, or help the blind, deaf, dumb, and leprous here in the world, in this transitory life?' Bultmann also interprets 'works' as being synonymous with 'words.' Understood in that sense, the greater works would refer to a greater ability to evangelise in the post resurrection era. It is worth noting that many Catholic commentators from the early Augustine onwards, would have agreed with Luther's interpretation.

As to the equation of words and works, Brown points out that Jesus said, 'the man who has faith in me will *perform* the same works as I *perform*.' The word 'perform' is used of deeds, not of words. Brown points out that while the word 'works' could certainly apply to healings and miracles – in this regard he refers to Mt 21:21; Mk 16:17-18; Acts 3:6; 9:34;40 – it would be true to say that in John there is less emphasis on the marvellous character of the greater works, than in the other gospels. When Brown refers to the marvellous deeds enumerated in the texts just cited, he says that the 'greater works' mentioned by John, 'are somewhat similar' to them. In the light of this carefully worded observation, it seems reasonable to suggest that the charism of faith is implicit in a proper understanding of Jn 14:12-14.

B) The Stilling of the Storm at Sea

The account of Jesus stilling the storm in Mt 8:24-28; Mk 4:35-41;

Lk 8:22-25, is the second text we will examine. Matthew's version which is derived like Luke's from Mark, reads as follows:

> He got into a boat and his disciples followed him. Suddenly a violent storm came up upon the sea, so that the boat was being swamped with waves; but he was asleep. They came and woke him saying, 'Lord save us! We are perishing!' He said to them, 'Why are you terrified, O you of little faith?' Then he got up, rebuked the winds and the sea, and there was a great calm. The men were amazed and said, 'What sort of man is this, whom even the winds and the sea obey?'

In one of his commentaries Meier, says that what may be involved here is an earthquake, which has a violent effect on the sea and the ship. He says that the storm is symbolic of the troubles of the church in times of crisis.[13] When the disciples panic, because they fear that the boat will sink, they wake up Jesus. Their cry for help, is tinged with an ambivalent attitude of rebuke and fearful trust as they call on Jesus to perform a miracle. He does so in an authoritative and effective way. In language reminiscent of his exorcisms, he 'rebukes' and 'muzzles' the storm. Immediately, the winds die down and calm returns. And then, instead of commending the disciples for relying on him in their hour of need, Jesus admonishes them because of their little faith. If it is accepted that Jesus is the model and exemplar of faith, it is possible that he was comparing the apostles lack of faith to his own superabundant confidence in God. What did he expect of the apostles? There are three possible answers.

> Firstly, that the disciples would have shown more confidence in Jesus when they woke him up. It should be said, however, that they did show considerable confidence in him. It is conveyed not only by the fact that they made their request, but in their mode of address, 'in Matthew it is a prayer for deliverance addressed to Jesus the *Kyrios*.'[14]
>
> Secondly, in Ps 107:23-32, sailors who were at their wits end during a storm. 'cried out to the Lord in their trouble, and God brought them out from their distress.' The disciples could have shown similar trust, by asking God with confi-

dence to enable them, either to ride out the storm without injury, or to bring it to an end as a result of a prayer of petition.

Thirdly, perhaps Jesus wanted the disciples to take heed of his teaching on mountain moving faith, and to say an authoritative word of command to the storm, in the belief that if there was no hesitation in their hearts, it would have been calmed.

By and large, options one and two involve trusting faith of the normal kind. In the light of the preceding analysis, the third option is not only plausible but likely. In other words what Jesus expected from the disciples, was the measure of *superabundant trust*, i.e. charismatic faith of an expectant kind. That, does not mean that contemporary believers are always supposed to exercise the charism of faith in situations of extreme difficulty. As was stated in the definition in chapter two, it is a *special* grace, given to some in *particular* situations. So while a person cannot expect to be granted the charism of faith in times of crisis, he or she can be open to that possibility.

C) Peter Walks on Water

The third text, we will examine, recalls how Peter walked for a time on water. It can be found in Mt 14:22-34; Mk 6:45-52: Jn 6:16-21. In the three accounts it is an epiphany story,[15] the only one in the gospels, where Jesus wills to reveal himself to the apostles in his transcendent majesty and power, by walking towards them across the water. Matthew's version includes a different ending. It reads as follows in 14:28-34:

> Peter answered him, 'Lord, if it is you, command me to come to you on the water.' He said, 'Come.' So Peter got out of the boat, started walking on the water, and came toward Jesus. But when he noticed the strong wind, he became frightened, and beginning to sink, he cried out, 'Lord save me!' Jesus immediately reached out his hand and caught him, saying to him, 'You of little faith, why did you doubt?' When they got into the boat, the wind ceased. And those in the boat worshipped him, saying, 'Truly you are the son of God.'

When Peter sees Jesus, he addresses him as Lord, and asks permission to share in his miraculous power over nature. He gave notional assent to the belief that with God all things are possible. But he seemed to know instinctively that unless his desire was in conformity with the will of God and his subsequent action was empowered by God, he would be unable to walk on water. Both were manifested when Jesus said 'come' in response to Peter's request. This one word, was the word of God, the word as a revelatory verb, the inspired invitation that leapt alive with meaning into Peter's heart thereby empowering him, like Jesus, the man of faith *par excellence,* to defy gravity and to walk on water. With a heart brimming with confidence, Peter stepped out of the boat and began to walk toward Jesus. But as his attention was distracted by wind and waves, he lost the power of the word that he has just heard, and began to sink. He cried out to Jesus, asking him to save him from death by drowning. The Lord stooped to help him, and immediately afterwards admonished him for his lack of faith, 'why did you doubt?' he asked. In a way this was a surprising question. When Peter cried out to Jesus, he did express his faith and trust in him. But it wasn't the 'measure' (cf. Rom 12:3) of faith that Jesus expected of him, the kind of superabundant trust that has 'no doubt in the heart' (cf. Mk 11:23). In other words, when Jesus said the word 'come,' Peter was granted the grace of charismatic faith. When that faith regressed, so to speak, to a lesser measure of trusting faith of a fearful kind, Jesus was disappointed. Just as in the previous story, the fact that Peter's trust in Jesus is shot through with fear, is a sign of a lack of confident faith. As Dulles has pointed out, in the synoptic gospels fear and doubt are the opposite to faith.[16]

Conclusion

At the end of this chapter we are in a position to come to a number of conclusions. Firstly, it is highly probable that Jesus spoke about the charism of faith when he promised believers that they would be able to move metaphorical mountains or mulberry trees of difficulty. Secondly, although the charism of faith is intimately associated with the charisms of healings and miracles in 1 Cor 12:9;28;30, it does not necessarily have to be. It can be operative either in a person who seeks ministry from someone else, or who is inspired to pray for some favour – not necessarily a healing or a miracle. By and large, the importance of this gift in the life and teaching of Jesus, seems to be underestimated by exegetes and theologians. However there is an obvious problem with this conclusion. It is clear from 1 Cor 12:9 that the charism of faith, like the other gifts listed in 1 Cor 12:8-10, is granted to *some* and not to *all* of the faithful. Nevertheless, it would appear that Jesus not only advocated this kind of faith as if it were normative, he expected to find it in the apostles and all those he ministered to. There is only one explanation – though admittedly not a very convincing one – that might resolve this dilemma. All those who lived in the messianic time of our Lord, may have been uniquely gifted with the charism of faith in virtue of their relationship with him.

CHAPTER SEVEN

The Charism of Faith in the Fathers of the Church and St Thomas

This chapter will examine what the Fathers of the Church and St Thomas Aquinas had to say, about the charism of faith. There is an enormous amount of published material that could be surveyed. Instead of trying to be comprehensive, we will look at representative texts that contain typical patristic and Thomistic attitudes to the charism. There are two main groups, those which interpret the charism primarily in *didactic* terms, i.e. as an inspired grasp of revealed truth that leads to effective preaching and teaching, and those which interpreted it primarily in *dynamic* terms as an inner certainty that leads to deeds of power such as healings and miracle working.

In the early centuries of Christian history, there is evidence to show that the church continued to exercise the charisms listed in 1 Cor 12:8-10. For example, around 160 A.D. St Ignatius of Antioch wrote to bishop Polycarp, praying that he might be, 'deficient in nothing and might abound in all the gifts.' Addressing believers in Smyrna he refers to the community as one 'that mercifully has obtained every kind of charism and is deficient in no gift.'[1] St Irenaeus (c. 130-202 A.D.) testified that, 'it is not possible to name the number of gifts which the church throughout the world has received from God.' In *Against Heresies* II, 49.3, he says:

> Some drive out demons really and truly, so that those cleansed from evil spirits believe and become members of the Church; some have foreknowledge of the future, visions, and prophetic utterances; others by the laying on of hands, heal the sick and restore them to health; and before now, as I said, dead men have actually been raised and have remained with us for many years. In fact, it is impossible to enumerate the gifts which throughout the world the Church has received from God and in the name of

> Jesus Christ who was crucified under Pontius Pilate, and every day puts to effectual use for the benefit of the heathen, deceiving no one and making profit out of no one: freely she received from God, and freely she ministers ... We hear of many members of the Church who have prophetic gifts and by the Spirit with all kinds of tongues, and bring men's secret thoughts to light for their own good, and expound the mysteries of God.[2]

So the gifts, including the charism of faith, were commonly experienced in the opening centuries of the Christian era. Later on however, they fell into abeyance due in part to the ritualisation of charisms and the struggle between the church and the Montanists. Not surprisingly, many of the Fathers of the Church, and sometime later, St Thomas, referred to the charism of faith. They often did so within the context of more general discussions of the charisms in 1 Cor 12:8-10, or while commenting on different passages in the scriptures. By and large their interpretations fell into two main categories, dynamic and didactic. In the dynamic view the charism of faith is primarily related to the following gifts of healings and miracle working, and only in a subordinate way to the preceding gifts of wisdom and knowledge. In the didactic view, however, the charism of faith is primarily related to the preceding gifts of wisdom and knowledge and only in a secondary and subordinate way to the following gifts of healing and miracle working.

The Charism of Faith as the Key to Deeds of Power

A) St John Chrysostom

Surprisingly, although St John Chrysostom lived in the post charismatic era, he expresses a charismatic point of view in his, *Homilies on the Epistles of Paul to the Corinthians*. Having spoken briefly about the gifts of wisdom and knowledge he goes on to describe the charism of faith in *dynamic terms*. Commenting on 1 Cor 12:9 he says:

> 'And to another faith,' not meaning by this the faith of doctrines, but the faith of miracles; concerning which Christ says, 'If you have faith as a grain of mustard seed, you will say to this mountain, "Move from here to there,"

> and it will move' Mt 17:20. And the apostles too concerning this besought him saying, 'Increase our faith' Lk 17:5, for this is the mother of the miracles. But to possess the power of working miracles and gifts of healing is not the same thing: for he that has a gift of healing used only to do cures: but he that possessed powers of working miracles used to punish also. For a miracle is not the only healing, but the punishing also: even as Paul inflicted blindness: and as Peter slew Ananias and Sapphira.[3]

There are a number of observations that can be made about this quotation. In general terms, it offers the classical charismatic interpretation. Firstly, instead of seeing faith in doctrinal terms it sees it as a separate charism. Secondly, in a graphic phrase, Chrysostom refers to the charism of faith as, the 'mother of miracles,' which typically expresses itself in mountain-moving deeds of power. Thirdly, in Chrysostom's estimation, the gift of faith in 1 Cor 12:9 is the same as the one spoken about by Christ in the gospels. This interpretation fits in with the perspective of many modern exegetes and charismatics.

John Chrysostom saw a connection between the mention of faith in 1 Cor 12:9 and some references to faith in the gospels. In a homily on Mt 17:19, he made the following points. They are worth quoting in a slightly edited way:

> The disciples came to Jesus privately and said, 'Why could we not cast it out?' Mt 17:19. It seems to me that they were anxious and fearful, that they had lost the grace with which they had been entrusted. For they received power over unclean spirits (Mt 10:1). Taking him aside they asked him about the reason for their failure … What did Christ reply? 'Because of your little faith. For Truly, I say to you, if you have faith as a grain of mustard seed, you will say to this mountain, 'move from here to there,' and it will move; and nothing will be impossible for you' Mt 17:20. Now if you say, 'Why did they not move a mountain?' I would reply, that in fact they did far greater things, having raised people from the dead. For it is one thing to move a mountain, it is quite another to give life to a dead body. And some of the saints, who weren't as great

as the apostles, are said to have actually moved mountains when there was a need for such action. The apostles would have done the same if it had been necessary. But there was no such need. So we can't find fault for them not doing so. And besides, Jesus himself hadn't said, 'you *will* move mountains,' but rather, 'you will *be able* to move mountains.' So if they didn't do any mountain moving, it wasn't due to lack of ability. They had the ability to do even greater things. It is just that the need didn't actually arise ... When Jesus speaks of faith here, he means the kind that works miracles. That is why he mentions the mustard seed of faith. He wants to convey its unspeakable power. For although the mustard seed is very small in size, it is unequalled in power. What Jesus is saying, is that even the smallest, but genuine amount of this kind of faith will be able to do great things. He went beyond the mustard seed, to mention the moving of mountains, and concluded by saying that nothing would be impossible to the person of faith.[4]

In this quotation, Chrysostom again affirms without compromise, his 'charismatic' interpretation of the gift of faith. It is clear that he believed that Jesus not only wanted his disciples to exercise this charism, he authorised and empowered them to do so.

We noted in chapter five, that many commentaries on Jn 14:8-15, explain the passage solely in terms of effective preaching and teaching. It is interesting to note what John Chrysostom had to say about these verses in the 'Homilies of St John.' True to his 'charismatic' understanding, he interprets Jn 14:8-15 in a literal way. He wrote:

Next, to show that not only could he do these works, but also others much greater than, he continued in exalted terms. For he did not merely say: 'I can perform even greater works than these,' but something much more remarkable. He declared: 'I can even grant to others to perform still greater works than these. Amen, amen, I say to you, he who believes in me, the works that I do he shall do, and greater than these shall he do, because I am going to the Father.' That is: 'In future the working of miracles is

> your prerogative because I am going away.' ... He said this to show that what he had said before was said with their weakness in mind. And the words, 'I am going to the Father,' have this meaning: 'I shall not disappear when I return to heaven, I will always remain with my followers.' He said these things to encourage them. For it was probable that, because they did not understand the Resurrection, they would consider his words as sad news. Therefore, because of his all embracing care for them, he promised that they would perform for others the same good works that he performed. By his word of reassurance he was indicating that he would not only remain with them always, he would display even greater power through them.[5]

Although Chrysostom doesn't mention the gift of faith in this passage, in view of what he has said already about the connection between the charism of faith and deeds of power, one can presume that it is implicit throughout. From what he says, it is possible, though unlikely, that he believed that this promise was made to the apostles, and not necessarily to subsequent generations.

B) St Cyril of Jerusalem

In one of his 'Catechetical Lectures,' St Cyril of Jerusalem (c. 315-386A.D.) mentions Mk 11:23 in the course of the most helpful and insightful Patristic passage on the charism of faith. Because of its importance and clarity we will quote it in its entirety.

> The word 'faith' has two meanings. First of all, it is concerned with doctrine and it denotes the assent of the soul to some truth. Faith in this sense brings blessing and salvation to the soul, as the Lord said, 'He who hears my word and believes him who sent me, has eternal life; he does not come to judgment' Jn 5:24, and again: 'He who believes in the Son is not judged, but has passed from death to life.' See how striking God's goodness is. He does not despise the long years of service given by his people, but what they achieved by many years of effort, Jesus now gives you in an instant as a free gift. For if only you believe that Jesus Christ is Lord, and that God raised him from the

dead, you will be saved, and he who gave a home in paradise to the thief will give you a home there also. Do not doubt the truth of what I say: after only a brief moment of faith the Lord saved the thief on our holy hill of Golgotha and he will save you too if you believe. The word 'faith' has a second meaning: it is a particular gift and grace of Christ. 'To one is given through the Spirit the utterance of wisdom, and to another the utterance of knowledge, according to the same Spirit, to another faith by the same spirit, to another gifts of healing' 1 Cor 12:8-9. Faith in the sense of a particular divine grace conferred by the Spirit is not primarily concerned with doctrine but with giving people powers which are quite beyond their capability. He who has this faith will say to the mountain, 'Move from here to there' Mk 11:23, and it will move, and anyone can in fact say these words through faith and believe without hesitation that they will come to pass, receives this particular grace. It is to this kind of faith that the Lord's words refer: 'If you have faith as a grain of mustard seed.' Now a mustard seed is small in size but its energy thrusts it upwards with the force of fire. Small are its roots, great the spread of its boughs, and once it is fully grown the birds of the air find shelter in its branches. So too in a flash, faith can produce the most wonderful effects in the soul ... Illumined by faith it gazes at the glory of God as far as human nature allows and going beyond the boundaries of the universe it has a vision, before the consummation of all things, of the judgment and of God, making good the rewards he promised. As far as it depends on you then, cherish the first gift of faith which leads you to God and you will receive the higher gift which no effort of yours can reach, no powers of yours attain.[6]

A number of comments can be made about this text. Clearly, Cyril comes down on the side of Chrysostom, by saying there are two kinds of faith, doctrinal and trusting. Firstly, he makes it clear that it is a particularly intense form of this second kind of faith, the type Paul mentions in 1 Cor 12:9. Secondly, he is convinced that Jesus had this kind of faith in mind when he talked to the apostles about their ability to move mountains. Thirdly, Cyril is well aware of the interrelationship of the two kinds of faith, and how the charism relies on, and indeed expresses the life of doctrinal faith. Fourthly, he seems to think that a person with strong justifying faith, can expect to be granted the special gift of charismatic faith. Fifthly, he adds a distinctive point when he says, that the gift of faith leads to an inner illumination of spirit, which enables the person to contemplate the glory of God and the consummation of all things in the end times. Evidently, there is an eschatological dimension to the charism of faith, as we noted in chapter three. This emphasis might help to explain why it is that only a minority of people are cured as a result of healing prayer. Such healings are a foretaste, of the transformation of all things in the second coming. The charism of faith is the Spirit-given spark that makes such manifestations and epiphanies possible.

C) Eusebius of Cesarea

Bishop Eusebius of Cesarea, provides two memorable examples of the kind of faith described by Sts John Chrysostom and Cyril of Jerusalem. They are recounted in his *The History of the Christian Church*. In one anecdote, reminiscent of the marriage feast of Cana, he recalls how during an Easter Vigil, the deacons ran out of lamp oil. The congregation was distressed. Then a saintly man called Narcissus, asked the deacons to bring him water. 'Then he said a prayer over the water, and instructed them to pour it into the lamps *with absolute faith in the Lord*.' They did his bidding and, 'in defiance of natural law, by the miraculous power of God, the substance of the liquid was changed from water into oil.' Eusebius concludes the story by saying that people kept small amounts of the oil that was left over, as proof of this wonderful event.

In the second, incident, a group of Christian soldiers were expiring as a result of thirst. 'But the soldiers of the Melitene Legion, as it is called, through faith which has never wavered from that day to this, as they faced the enemy in their lines, knelt down on the ground, our normal attitude when praying, and turned to God in supplication. The enemy was astonished at the sight. But the record goes on to say that something more astonishing followed a moment later: a thunderbolt drove the enemy to flight and destruction, while rain fell on the army which had called on the Almighty, reviving it when the entire force was on the point of perishing of thirst.'[7]

There is yet another example in the life of St Anthony. A man whose daughter was troubled by an evil spirit, came to him seeking help. Anthony said, 'I am a man like you. But if you believe in Christ whom I serve, go, and according as you believe, pray to God, and it will come to pass.' Straightaway, therefore he departed, *believing* and calling on Christ, and he found his daughter had been cleansed of the devil.[8]

The Charism of Faith as the Key to Doctrinal Knowledge

Besides the dynamic interpretation of 1 Cor 12:9 there is another. It could be referred to as the didactic view. It was expressed by Fathers of the Church, and later by St Thomas. They were writing in the post charismatic era.

A) Origen

John Clark Smith says in, that in his dispute with Celsus – who maintained that the Christians only converted ignorant people – Origen (c. 185- c. 254 A.D.) wanted to show the relationship of faith, to wisdom and knowledge. To do so he chose 1 Cor 12:9 which he interpreted in a didactic rather than in a dynamic way. He wrote:

> So divine wisdom, which is not the same thing as faith, is first of what are called spiritual gifts of God; the second place after it, for those who have an accurate understanding of these matters, is held by what is called knowledge; and faith stands in the third place, since salvation must be available also for the simple folk who advance in religion as far as they can. This is the way Paul has it in 1 Cor 12:8-9.[9]

It is clear from this quotation that Origen did not interpret the charism of faith in terms of the kind of intense trust that leads to deeds of power. That said it is not entirely clear whether he saw the charism of faith as kerygmatic instruction, justifying faith, or a combination of the two.

B) Hillary of Poitiers

In his life of St Honaratus, Hillary of Poitiers (c. 315-367 A.D.), described the charism of faith primarily in *didactic terms*:

> For the gift of the Spirit is manifest, where wisdom makes utterance and the words of life are heard, and where there is knowledge that comes from God-given insight, lest after the fashion of beasts through the ignorance of God we should fail to know the Author of our life, or by faith in God, lest by not believing the Gospel of God, we should be outside the gospel; or by the gift of healings; that by the cure of diseases we should bear witness to his grace who bestows these things; or by the working of miracles, that what we do may be understood to be the power of God.[10]

Once again, there are a number of observations worth making about this quotation. It seems clear that Hillary did not have any direct experience of the charisms in 1 Cor 12:8-10. As a result, he introduces, the classic non-charismatic, interpretation of the text. Firstly, he understands the charism of faith in a didactic way, as a reference to doctrinal faith. Secondly, although he accepts that healings and miracles can occur, it logically follows, that instead of seeing the charism of faith expressing itself primarily in such deeds of power, he relates it primarily to the charisms of wisdom and knowledge. Later in the same passage he interprets the gift of prophesy as 'understanding of doctrine.' Thirdly, because of his doctrinal interpretation of faith, he sees no connection between the gift of faith in 1 Cor 12:9 and any of the sayings of Jesus, e.g. in Mt 17:20 or Mk 11:23. Although, Hillary's understanding of the charism of faith is questionable from an exegetical and an experiential point of view, it became the predominant one over a period of time. His interpretation, rather than that of John Chrysostom and Cyril of Jerusalem, was reflected in the teaching of St Thomas Aquinas, and through him, in most of subsequent Catholic thinking on the subject. One could say that this interpretation marked the final triumph of the Greek understanding of faith as mental assent to revealed truth over the Hebrew understanding of faith as heartfelt trust in God and the promises of God.

C) St Thomas Aquinas

St Thomas Aquinas epitomised the Scholastic attitude to this particular charism, when he understood it principally in terms of Origen's and Hillary of Poitier's didactic perspective. We will begin by situating Thomas's interpretation of 1 Cor 12:9 within the general context of his theology of faith. His major treatise on the virtue of faith is to be found in the *Summa Theologiae*. There are many modern studies which examine his thinking on this subject.

Thomas lived in an age when attention was mainly focused on the gifts of the Spirit mentioned in Is 11:2, which reads: 'On him will rest the spirit of Yahweh, the spirit of wisdom and insight, the spirit of counsel and power, the spirit of knowledge and fear of Yahweh.' In the *Summa,* St Thomas describes these gifts in great detail, and relates them in a brilliant way, to the virtues, beatitudes and fruits of the Spirit.[11] It is clear that he valued them highly. However, Thomas was also interested in the gifts of the Spirit, including the charism of faith, mentioned in 1 Cor 12:8-10. He wrote a good deal about them in his two theological masterpieces, The *Summa Theologiae* and the *Summa Contra Gentiles*, and also in his biblical commentaries, especially those on 1 Corinthians and Matthew's Gospel. We will look briefly at some relevant aspects of his thinking on the charisms, especially the charism of faith.

One baptism many infillings

In one significant passage, St Thomas links charismatic activity with in-fillings of the Spirit. Having asked whether a person who received the Holy Spirit in baptism could receive subsequent in-fillings (cf. Eph 5:18), he responded in the affirmative. He said that with each new outpouring, the Spirit *lives* in us in a new way, in order that we may be empowered to *do* new things, which may or may not be 'charismatic.'[12] He wrote:

> There is an invisible sending of grace with respect to an advance in virtue or an increase in grace ... Such an invisible sending is especially to be seen in the kind of increase of grace whereby a person moves forward into some new act, or some new state of grace: as, for instance, when a person moves forward *into the grace of working miracles, or*

> *of prophecy*, or out of burning love of God offers his life as a martyr, or renounces all his possessions, or undertakes any arduous work.[13]

St Thomas goes on to say that the sendings of the Holy Spirit do not *intensify* grace, but rather *extend* its influence.[14] This teaching is consistent with what we read in the Acts of the apostles. Having received the Holy Spirit on Pentecost (cf Acts 2:1-14) the disciples experienced another outpouring of the same Spirit when they were facing persecution. Acts 4:31 describes what happened: 'As they prayed, the house where they were assembled, rocked. From this time they were all filled with the Holy Spirit and began to proclaim the word of God fearlessly.'

The gifts of the Spirit

St Thomas described the gifts mentioned in 1 Cor 12:8-10. We can concentrate on what he had to say in his two *Summas* and in his biblical commentary, firstly about the charisms of wisdom and knowledge, secondly, about the charism of faith, and thirdly about the charisms of healing and miracle working. We can begin with two general observations. Speaking about the list of charisms in 1 Cor 12:8-10 St Thomas says that Paul distinguishes between graces, offices and activities. 'A gift of *grace*, confers a certain power, for example, the power of prophesy or to perform miracles, etc. The authority to exercise such powers come from some *office*, for example, from apostleship, etc. To exercise such power authoritatively pertains to the realm of *action*.'[15] He considers the charisms – within the general context of an examination of gratuitous graces. Whereas, sanctifying grace, 'ordains a man immediately to a union with his last end,'[16] he says that gratuitous grace 'is ordained to this, that a person may help another to be led to God.'[17] In other words, sanctifying grace is given to help the recipient grow in holiness, whereas gratuitous grace is given in order to help others to grow in the same holiness. St Thomas then goes on to say that the sanctification of others is made possible by 'instructing them in divine things.' To do this effectively, a person needs three things, right knowledge, communication skills, and persuasive proof. Consistent with his intellectualist approach to faith, Thomas believes that right knowledge is of primary importance.

The gifts/charisms of wisdom and knowledge

He saw the gifts of wisdom and knowledge, as a graced means of having an intuitive, or quasi instinctive rapport with the divine mind and will. St Thomas describes this kind of connatural knowledge as an ability:

> To judge well about the things of God through a certain oneness in nature with God is an act of the Spirit's gift of wisdom. Such sympathy or connaturality with divine things is an effect of the love of charity uniting us to God, so that wisdom's cause is love in the will, even if in essence wisdom is a disposition of mind to judge well. The gift of understanding guides the mind's perceptions, but the gifts of wisdom and knowledge form its judgments[18] … Understanding is more excellent than wisdom as an intellectual virtue, since it attains to God more intimately by a kind of union of the soul with Him, it is able to direct us not only in contemplation, but also in action.[19]

Although St Thomas tends to be very objective in his theology, he is nevertheless, aware of the subjective effects of a growth in wisdom and knowledge. He says: 'now perception implies a certain *experimental knowledge* called wisdom, as it were a *sweet knowledge*.'[20]. This kind of experiential knowing enables a person to speak effectively, i.e. by means of the charismatic word, or utterance of wisdom and knowledge. The gift of *wisdom* according to Thomas is 'knowledge of divine things' The gift of *knowledge* is 'knowledge of human things.'[21]

Needless to say, he was well aware that wisdom and knowledge are two of the seven gifts of the Holy Spirit mentioned in Is 11:2. As such they are supernatural graces. Why then, he asks, are wisdom and knowledge in 1 Cor 12:8, gratuitous graces? His reply is interesting:

> They are numbered among the gratuitous graces, in as much as they imply such a fullness of knowledge and wisdom that a person may not merely think aright of Divine things, but may instruct others and overpower adversaries.[22]

In a fascinating passage, Thomas describes some inspired ways in which wisdom and knowledge can grow:

> Now, accompanying this light that we have mentioned (i.e. of the virtue of faith) which illumines the mind from within, there are at times in divine revelation other external or internal aids to knowledge; for instance, a spoken message, or something heard by the external senses which is produced by divine power, or something perceived internally through imagination due to God's action, or also some things produced by God that are seen in bodily visions, or that are internally pictured in the imagination. From these presentations, by the light internally impressed on the mind, man receives a knowledge of divine things. Consequently, without the interior light, these aids do not suffice for a knowledge of divine things, but the interior light does suffice without them.[23]

The Charism of Faith

Thomas believed that the unusual certainty associated with charismatic faith was rooted in the gifts of wisdom and knowledge. He says that the charism of faith is:

> Enumerated here under the gratuitous graces, not as a virtue justifying man himself, but *as implying a super-eminent certitude of faith,* whereby a person is fitted for instructing others concerning such things as belong to the faith.[24]

In his biblical commentary on 1 Cor 12:9 Thomas adds:

> 'To another faith [is given] by the same Spirit.' But this faith is not to be understood as the theological virtue of faith, for that is common to all the members of Christ (cf. Heb 11:6) It is, rather, to be understood either as the expression of faith, whereby, a person can correctly present those things which are of the faith, or as the certitude of faith, which some have in a more excellent way, as Jesus says to the Canaanite woman in Mt 15:28, 'O woman, great is your faith!'[25]

In other words, the sanctifying effect of the virtue of faith leads to a kind of certitude about revealed truth. The charism of faith, however, leads some people to have *a super-eminent certitude* about such truths that results in an unusual ability to impart them to others.

The charisms of healing and miracle working

Thomas also examines the gifts of healing and miracle working.[26] He says: 'The grace of healing is mentioned separately (from that of miracles) because by it's means a benefit, namely bodily health, is conferred on man in addition to the common benefit bestowed in all miracles, namely the bringing of men to the knowledge of God.' Thomas also examines the gift of miracle working. He says: 'Two things may be considered in miracles. One is that which is done: this is something surpassing the faculty of nature, and in this respect miracles are called virtues. The other thing is the purpose for which miracles are wrought, namely the manifestation of something supernatural, and in this respect they are commonly called signs, but on account of some excellence they receive the name of wonder or prodigy, as showing something from afar.'[27]

The gifts are described within a didactic framework. The one who speaks about revealed things, which 'surpass knowledge' of a merely rational kind, needs to confirm the truth of what has been said, by means of healings and miracles. He writes:

> Now just as the knowledge which man receives from God needs to be brought to the knowledge of others through the ... grace of the word, so the word uttered needs to be confirmed in order that it be rendered credible.[28]

A number of observations can be made about Thomas's understanding of deeds of power. Firstly, he saw the charism of faith, first and foremost as super-eminent certitude of a *doctrinal* kind and only secondarily as a graced ability to perform deeds of power. It was an understanding, which as we have seen, owed more to the didactic views of Origen and Hillary of Poitiers than to the dynamic perspective of John Chrysostom and Cyril of Jerusalem. That said, Thomas says more than once that the deeds of power which confirm the word, are rooted in faith, presumably trusting faith of the expectant unhesitating kind. A couple of quotations will illustrate the point. In an article entitled 'Whether there is a gratuitous grace of working miracles?' he says:

> The working of miracles results from faith, – either of the worker, according to 1 Cor 13:2, 'If I should have all faith, so as I could move mountains,' or of other persons for whose sake miracles are wrought, according to Mt 13:58, 'And he wrought not many miracles there, because of their unbelief.' Therefore, if faith be reckoned a gratuitous grace, it is superfluous to reckon in addition the working of signs as another gratuitous grace.[29]

A little later, in typical style, St Thomas gives his response to this objection, and it is interesting because of what it says about the charism of faith and miracle working:

> The working of miracles is ascribed to faith for two reasons. First, because it is directed to the confirmation of faith; secondly, because it proceeds from God's omnipotence on which faith relies. Nevertheless, just as besides the grace of faith, the grace of the word is necessary that people may be instructed in the faith, so too is the grace of miracles necessary that people may be confirmed in their faith.[30]

Because St Thomas made the charism of faith the keystone in the theological bridge of gratuitous graces, the whole edifice is undermined once his understanding of that charism is questioned. His mainly didactic interpretation of the charism of faith has to be questioned from a scriptural and experiential point of view. In so far as this is the case, his understanding of the other gifts would have to be revised. As Morton Kelsey rightly points out, it is highly unlikely that Jesus' primary motive for performing deeds of power was to confirm the truth of what was being preached.[31] Surely, when he prayed with faith for the healing of the sick he was motivated by Christian compassion.

Conclusion

This chapter has indicated that, as far as the charism of faith was concerned, the Fathers of the Church had two main views. John Chrysostom and Cyril of Jerusalem maintained that it was a prerequisite for the performance of deeds of power. Origen and Hillary of Poitiers, however saw the charism as an unusually clear insight into the mysteries of faith and an ability to impart that insight in a saving way. St Thomas tended to interpret the charism of faith mainly in a didactic, rather than in a dynamic way, as an exceptionally certain grasp of the truths of faith which were imparted to others with exceptional conviction and efficacy. It was primarily rooted in the gifts of wisdom and knowledge, and only expressed itself in a secondary and subordinate way by means of the other charisms including the charisms of healing and miracle working. Thomas's theology has had a great deal of influence on Catholic attitudes to the charisms mentioned by Paul in 1 Cor 12:8-10. Though insightful and cogent, Thomas's understanding of the charism of faith can be a bit misleading. It needs to be revised in the light of modern scripture scholarship, the teachings of the Second Vatican Council, and the experience of the contemporary Pentecostal and Charismatic movements.

CHAPTER EIGHT

Modern Charismatics and the Charism of Expectant Faith

Up to now the emphasis has been on scripture. At this point it shifts to the experience and writings of twentieth century Charismatics. At the outset of this chapter it is necessary from a methodological point of view to posit a principle of continuity and discontinuity. There is continuity between the experience of modern Charismatics and those in the New Testament and post New Testament era. This would mean for example, that it is likely that there is continuity between the charismatic experiences described by Paul in 1 Cor 12:8-10, e.g. speaking in tongues, and those of contemporary Charismatics.

However, there is also a principle of discontinuity at work. Religious experiences like other experiences occur within a particular historical and cultural context which influences the way they occur. That same context also exerts a significant influence on the way in which they are understood and articulated. Clearly, there is a considerable difference between the ethos of the New Testament era, and that of the late twentieth century. Furthermore, there are other more nuanced differences between religious experiences that occur nowadays within a Catholic or a Protestant environment. It is arguable that down the ages there has been a considerable continuity of *faith* experience, while at the same time there has been a discontinuity in the articulation of that faith experience in terms of *beliefs*.

All of this is important when it comes to a study of the lives and literature of contemporary Charismatics, who have written about the charism of faith. Unlike the Fathers of the Church who wrote by and large in an impersonal objective way, modern Charismatics tend to augment their objective understanding of God's word with their experience of the out-working of that same word in their own lives. We will take an extended look at Kathryn Kuhlman,a Protestant, who was described in 1970 by *Time Magazine* as a 'walking Lourdes,' and then a briefer look at the writings of Francis McNutt a Catholic. When we read what they said about the charism of faith, we can try at the same time to appreciate the expression of their different views in terms of the conditioning factors that have effected them. For example, as a Baptist with strong Pentecostal leanings, Kuhlman was strongly influenced by a trusting rather than a doctrinal approach to faith. While McNutt also emphasises trust, he has a strong grounding in the critical attitudes of philosophy, theology and modern exegesis, mainly of the Catholic kind.

Kathryn Kuhlman

From an early age Kathryn Kuhlman felt called to be an evangelist. Her ministry and theology had been influenced by the career of Aimee Semple McPherson, of the Assemblies of God, who was notorious for her flamboyant style, and her emphasis on the healing power of the Spirit. Apparently, Kathryn had briefly attended McPherson's Bible school, called the Lighthouse of International Foursquare Evangelism. It seems that she didn't fit in too well, and was asked to leave before completing her course. She also attended Simpson Bible Institute, where she failed the preaching exam and was finally expelled for unbecoming behaviour.

In her early years, Kathryn ministered at first with her sister and brother-in-law. Later she developed her own itinerant ministry. She went from place to place preaching the gospel, and invited people to accept Jesus as their personal Lord and Saviour. In the early thirties, at the height of the depression, she ministered in the Denver Revival Tabernacle, which had a sign erected above the building which declared in large letters, 'Prayer Changes Things.' While she was there she experienced the first defining episode of her life.

In 1935, Kathryn met an evangelist called Burroughs A. Waltrip whom she always referred to as 'Mister'. In the minds of many he was a personification of Sinclair Lewis's Elmer Gantry.[1] He was married with two children, good-looking, an eloquent speaker, and a lover of money and reputation. In spite of these facts, Kathryn fell in love with him. Waltrip eventually left his wife and his children. In 1938, contrary to the entreaties of many friends and her own misgivings, Kathryn married him. For a number of years she lived with Mister and ministered with him. But eventually she acknowledged that she was living a lie. As Prov 28:13 says, 'No one who conceals transgressions will prosper, but one who confesses and forsakes them will obtain mercy.' Like a latter day prodigal, she came to her senses literally at the dead end of a Los Angeles street. She described her anguish as follows: 'I knew nothing about the wonderful infilling of the Holy Spirit, I knew nothing of the power of the mighty third person of the Trinity which was available to all. I just knew it was four o'clock on Saturday afternoon and I had come to the place in my life where I was ready to give up everything – even Mister – and die. I said it out loud, 'Dear Jesus, I surrender all. I give it all to you. Take my body. Take my heart. All I am is yours. I place it in your wonderful hands.[2]

A few days later she waited to board a train in Los Angeles. Burroughs who also knew that their relationship was not within the will of God, said to her, 'You will never see me again, I will not interfere with your life or your ministry.' They were prophetic words. They never did meet again. In 1970, however, Kathryn received a Valentine's Day card from her ex-husband. It brought tears to her eyes and she declared, 'No one will ever know what this ministry has cost me. Only Jesus.' Later in her career, when she was asked why God had chosen a woman to carry out the ministry of healing in such an effective way, Kathryn replied, 'perhaps it was because no man was prepared to pay the price.' When she said this, she seemed to refer to that fateful day when she said good-bye forever to Waltrip.

When she left Burroughs, Kathryn went to a town in northwestern Pennsylvania. There her ministry blossomed anew in the Franklin Gospel Tabernacle, but with greater power and authority than ever. During this time she occasionally attended services conducted by other evangelists. She was appalled and distressed by the unscrupulous approach of some of them. They tried to whip people into a frenzy of expectation and when they weren't healed, they blamed them for their lack of faith. She wrote sometime later: 'Too often I had seen pathetically sick people dragging their tired, weakened bodies home from a healing service, having been told that they were not healed simply because of their own lack of faith. My heart ached for these people, as I know how they struggled, day after day, trying desperately to obtain *more* faith, taking out that which they had, and trying to analyse it, in a hopeless effort to discover its deficiency which was presumably keeping them from the healing power of God.'[3]

This inaugurated another defining moment in Kuhlman's life. She was plunged into a period of soul searching. She prayed to God with longing and tears, and asked for enlightenment. What was the role of faith? Was it something that the individual could produce in him or herself? Was it dependent on one's personal goodness? Was it a reward given to those who serve the Lord? In whom did faith reside? The person who was sick? The person conducting the healing service? The congregation? Or a combination of all three?

During a time of intense bible study she came across the Isiahian passage which says 'He was wounded for our transgressions, bruised for our iniquities, and by his stripes we are healed' Is 53:5 and Pt 2:24. This messianic text confirmed her belief that Jesus came as saviour and healer, even if it didn't sort out the precise role of faith in healing. After this realisation she began to preach about the role of the Holy Spirit in Christian belief and in Christian living. During one inspired and inspiring sermon she concluded, 'Every church should be experiencing the miracles of Pentecost. Every church should be seeing the healings of the Book of Acts. The gift is for all of us.'[4] The next evening a woman asked to speak. She said that as she had listened to Miss Kuhlman speak the previous day, she had been healed of a tumour. It had happened without any prayer being said or the laying on of hands. Later that same week, Kathryn told her listeners that physical healing was just as possible as spiritual salvation. As she spoke, a man in the congregation called Orr was healed of a corneal injury which had left him blind in his right eye.[5] These events proved to be a turning point in Kuhlman's life. She wrote: 'I understood why there was no need for a healing line; no healing virtue in a card or a personality; no necessity for wild exhortations 'to have faith'.[6] From then on, she not only preached the good news of salvation in Christ, she expected the Lord to demonstrate his saving love by healing the sick. Although she never made this distinction, it seems clear that she believed that just as the word salvation is a two sided coin with redemption on one side and healing on the other, so faith was also a two sided coin with justifying faith on one side and charismatic faith on the other.

As the years passed Kuhlman developed an unusual type of healing ministry. Instead of praying for individuals with the laying on of hands, she relied instead on what Pentecostal Oral Roberts referred to as the 'word of knowledge' 1 Cor 12:8. Some people thought it was some kind of psychic ability such as clairvoyance. In terms of Catholic theology, however, it seemed to have been a form of knowledge of an infused kind, which enabled her to know who in the congregation was being healed of what illness.[7] She expressed her experience in these words: 'My mind is so surrendered to the Spirit, that I know the exact body being healed: the sickness, the affliction, and in some instances, the very sin in their lives. And yet I could not pretend to tell you *why* or *how*.'[8]

This gift was and still remains a controversial one. But what can be said, is that Kathryn believed that it enabled her to be guided by the Spirit, and to discern the will of God. This is a vital point in Kathryn's understanding of the charism of faith. It is only granted by God, when the person desires to act in accordance with the purposes of God. If Kathryn didn't know why or how she intuited what the Lord was doing, she was sure of two things. 'I had nothing to do with what was happening, and second, I *knew* that it was the supernatural power of Almighty God.'

Year after year, thousands of people attended her increasingly interdenominational services in places such as First Presbyterian Church in Pittsburgh, and the Shrine Auditorium in Los Angeles. Before she went on stage, Kathryn would ask God, sometimes with tears and sighs, to anoint her once again with the power of the Holy Spirit, for without such an anointing she would be unable to do anything.[9] Then she would preach, often for over an hour, until she was sure that the Spirit had overshadowed her. It was then, and only then that Kathryn would call out one healing after another. Often at the same instant, the people she had mentioned, would feel the healing power of God coming upon them. Ushers would invite them to go forward to the stage to bear witness to what God was doing for them. When those who had been blessed got to the stage Kathryn would ask them to tell their stories. Then she would pray, and they would usually be 'slain in the Spirit' and fall back on the stage.[10] By the time she died, it was estimated that thousands if not tens of thousands of people had received healings as a result of her ministry.

At this point we can take a close look at what Kathryn had to say about the charism of faith. It is mainly contained in two short sections of her many writings.[11] The first point worth making is the fact that Miss Kuhlman firmly rejected the appellation of 'faith healer'. It would seem that she did so because it implied that she was endowed with some healing power, something that she always denied. That said, she probably had a keener appreciation of the role of faith in deeds of power such as healing than any of her contemporaries. Hers was an experiential rather than a mainly theoretical knowledge.

She said on more than one occasion that it is as hard to define the gift of faith as it is to define the mysteries of time or energy. She maintained that it was easier to say what faith was not. It was not presumption. It is worth quoting her insightful remarks on this subject: 'There are many who mix the ingredients of their own mental attitude with a little confidence, a little pinch of trust, a generous handful of religious egoism, quote some scripture, add some desire – then mix it all together and label it "faith".'[12]

A) Faith is not notional belief

The gift of faith is not belief. The word 'belief' has become synonymous with mental assent to some truth, promise of scripture, or church teaching. But as Kathryn observes: 'You can believe a promise and at the same time not have the faith to appropriate that promise. But we have formed the habit of trying to appropriate by belief, forgetting that belief is a mental quality … while faith is from God.'[13] In this sense Kathryn is saying that real faith is more than belief or trust of the hesitant kind. Her use of language is not only confusing but unjustifiable. She sometimes reserves the word faith in an arbitrary way, for the kind that does deeds of power. That said, if one gets behind her words, to her experience and intent, what she says is very challenging indeed.

B) Faith and power

Kathryn says that faith is not powerless. She writes: 'You cannot have faith without results any more than you can have motion without movement. The thing we sometimes call faith is only trust, but although we trust in the Lord, it is *faith* which has action and power.'[14] A number of comments are in order here. Kathryn hadn't a trained analytical mind. As a result she sometimes failed to find the right words for her meaning. Clearly, however, she said that the kind of faith she has in mind is different from justifying and trusting faith of the wishful kind. By implication it must be expectant faith, characterised by inner conviction of a heartfelt, unhesitating kind. It also seems clear that hers was a faith, not so much in a static God who *exists*, but rather in a dynamic God who *acts* in a powerful way in accordance with his loving and compassionate inspirations and promises.

C) The nature of true faith

Kathryn does try to describe what the charism of faith actually is. Firstly, paraphrasing Heb 11:1, she says, 'Faith is that quality or power by which the things desired become the things possessed.'[15] Implicit in this definition is the interplay between past and future which is mentioned in texts such as Mk 11:23-24 and 1 Jn 5:14-16. If a person is convinced in the present, that a scripture promise is going to be fulfilled, it will be. In another place she said: 'Faith is more than belief. It is more than confidence. It is more than trust. It is more than the sum total of these things ... Faith as God himself imparts it to the heart, is spiritual. It's warm. It's vital. It lives. It throbs. Its power is absolutely irresistible when it is imparted to the heart by the Lord ... Heart belief is faith. Mind belief is nothing more than deep desire combined with mental assent.'[16]

Secondly, she asserts that the faith she speaks about is a grace, a free gift of the Lord. It is not acquired by good works, acts of service or heroic self-sacrifice. Kathryn says with disarming simplicity, but great insight, 'You do not pray for faith; you seek the Lord, and faith will come.'[17] Kathryn says that charismatic faith is not the result of effort of a subjective, self-absorbed kind. Paradoxically, it is when, we forget about ourselves and concentrate on the Lord, by means of contemplative attention, that faith is *evoked* in the heart. 'Look up,' says Kathryn, 'and see Jesus! He is your faith, He is our faith. It is not faith that you must seek, but Jesus.'[18] She says that faith is often compromised, as it was for the apostles during the storm on the lake, by looking at God in the light of the problem, rather than looking at the problem in the light of heartfelt relationship with God.

Thirdly, Kathryn endorses the biblical view that a mustard seed of genuine faith is enough to move a mountain. If nothing happens she says, it must be that what we thought was faith was not faith at all (i.e. charismatic faith). All that is needed is a small amount of the genuine gift. When it is present, God's power is made available. She wrote: 'One thing I know, in you and in me apart from God, there are no ingredients and *no* qualities which, however mixed or combined, will create even so much as a mustard seed of Bible faith.'[19]

E) The ease of faith

Fourthly, genuine faith is peaceful, effortless and authoritative. She points to the example of Jesus. In his case there was no groaning, no long drawn out battle. He spoke, and immediately the exorcism, healing or miracle occurred. Kathryn comments, 'With faith there is no struggle.' Then speaking about her own experience she adds: 'There have been times when I have felt faith so permeate every part of my being, that I have dared to say and do things which, had I leaned on my own understanding or reason, I would never have done. Yet it flowed through every word and act with such irresistible power that I literally stood in wonder at the mighty works of the Lord.'[20]

In chapter two, it was suggested that there are four elements in the New Testament depiction of faith; acknowledgement of need; hearing the good news; expectant trust and confession of faith. Although Kathryn said more than once that she couldn't detect any laws or constants in the healing ministry, the four points mentioned above were evident in her ministry.

> Although some men and women came to her services because of admiring or sceptical curiosity, most people attended because they were consciously aware that they, or someone they cared about, had a spiritual, psychological or physical *need*.
>
> Kathryn made sure that they heard God's anointed *word*, by preaching the message of salvation, often at great length, and speaking inspired words of knowledge.
>
> Her preaching usually evoked *faith* in the hearts of the listeners. But even if those who needed a blessing hadn't faith themselves, either the faith of Kathryn a relative, neighbour or friend sufficed.
>
> Finally, when people were healed, they were invited to *confess* their faith by coming up on stage to witness verbally to what God had done for them. So despite the obvious differences, there were certain aspects of Kathryn's healing services which could be traced back to the scriptures.

Shortly before her death, Kathryn was invited to speak to 4,000 students and staff at Oral Roberts University. She knew that she was suffering from serious heart disease. In the course of her talk she spoke about herself and the Holy Spirit. She acknowledged that God had acted powerfully through her and other people. But she added: 'There is more, so much more.' Then she concluded by saying: 'The world called me a fool for having given my entire life to the One whom I've never seen. I know exactly what I'm going to say when I stand in His presence. When I look upon that wonderful face of Jesus, I'll have just one thing to say: I tried. I gave myself the best I knew how. My redemption will have been perfected when I stand and see Him who made it all possible.'[21]

In the sight of the world Kathryn may have lived like a fool, but in the words of Paul she was a fool for Christ's sake. She died of heart failure in 1976 at the age of sixty eight. These words were inscribed on her grave, 'I believe in miracles because I believe in God, February 20, 1976.' Later that year a memorial plaque was erected in her hometown. It read, 'Kathryn Kuhlman.

Birthplace – Concordia Missouri, member of the Baptist Church, ordained minister of the Evangelical Church Alliance. Known for her belief in the Holy Spirit.' These succinct inscriptions summed up the career, and marked the passing of one of the most remarkable women of faith in the twentieth century.

Francis McNutt

Francis McNutt, was one of the best known and influential healers in the early years of the Catholic Charismatic Renewal. He has acknowledged that he was influenced by the late Agnes Sanford a Protestant, who wrote an influential book entitled *The Healing Light*. He wrote: 'Mrs Sanford ... is perhaps more responsible than anyone else for renewing the healing ministry in the main-line churches.'[22] McNutt, a Dominican priest at the time, met her in the mid sixties, when he attended a workshop on healing that she was conducting. He also attended some of Kathryn Kuhlman's services and spoke to her about the healing ministry. Having experienced baptism in the Spirit, this Doctor of Theology began to exercise the healing ministry, by praying for individuals as Agnes Sanford would do, and also in ever larger healing services as Kathryn Kuhlman would do. By the early seventies, Francis McNutt was by far the best known healer in the Catholic Church. At the height of his fame he wrote an influential book entitled *Healing* which was first published in 1974. From the point of view of this chapter it contains two relevant sections entitled, 'The Faith to be Healed,' and 'The Mystery of Faith,'[23] in which he describes, in a clear and cogent way, his understanding of the charism of faith.

Like Kathryn Kuhlman, McNutt understands faith mainly in terms of trust. He is clear about the fact that the charism of faith is different from the virtue of faith. He describes it in these words: 'As I understand it, the "gift of faith" is a ministry gift which God imparts to help us to pray with confidence and "no hesitation in our hearts" for a given intention. Since this confidence can come only by God's revealing his will at a given moment, the gift of "the word of knowledge" is closely connected with the "gift of faith".'[24]

A) Faith and the word and will of God

This is a good description of what informed members of the Charismatic Renewal would mean when they refer to the charism of faith. While, it is true that the will of God can be revealed by means of a 'word of Knowledge,' it can also be revealed in other ways. Although, McNutt says that the gift is given to a person who is praying for 'a given intention,' he like Kuhlman has healing in mind. He goes on immediately to say, after the quotation above, that through the word of knowledge, God indicates that he wants to heal 'a particular person.' But as we have seen in previous chapters, the gift of faith is not necessarily associated with healing, nor indeed with the person praying. Sometimes it is the person being prayed for, or even a third party who is graced with the gift. McNutt acknowledges this a number of times. For example, he writes: 'Just as a minister of healing may receive a "gift of faith" to trust in a private revelation and to pray the prayer of command, so a sick person may receive a genuine inspiration to believe that he, or she, has been healed, sometimes in spite of remaining symptoms. For them, obedience to their inner prompting seems to be the condition for their healing taking place.'[25]

B) Faith is God centered

Secondly, McNutt, says that this kind of trust is a matter of having faith in God, rather than having faith in one's faith.[26] In saying this he echoes the teaching of Kathryn Kuhlman who warned against the dangers of self-absorption. He says four points are involved here. We turn trustfully to the all knowing, all loving God who has the power to satisfy our deepest needs. We accept our doubts, but do not dwell on them. We put into action what faith we have, by praying for some particular intention. And finally, we leave the results to God.

C) Faith as intimate union with Christ

Thirdly, McNutt says that by means of the charism of faith, the soul enjoys close union with the mind, and loving will of Christ. If a person has to pray in a conditional way with trusting faith, he or she speaks *to* God "out there" and asks for a blessing. If the person can pray the prayer of command with confidence and authority, he or she prays *with* Christ, to God. In *Healing* he writes: 'To pray in the name of Jesus means to pray *in the person of Jesus* – as Jesus himself would pray. To pray in the name of Jesus means that we must put on "that mind which was in Christ Jesus," that we see people and situations as Jesus does, and then speak with the power and authority of Jesus.'[27] Although McNutt doesn't develop this point, it is an important one.

When one reads what Charismatics say about the charism of faith, it seems to involve elements of what Catholics traditionally referred to as the illuminative and intuitive stages of the Christian life. Charismatic faith is a form of spiritual illumination in so far as it discerns in an existential as opposed to a notional way, what the will of God might be in a particular situation. As we have seen, the intuitive word of knowledge is one of the unusual ways in which it can occur. Sometimes, however a person praying from the heart for another, suddenly realises that his or her compassionate concern is a share in the compassionate disposition of Christ himself. When the one praying experiences this kind of spiritual and affective union with the Lord, it not only reveals the loving will of God in an existential way, it evokes at the same time, the inner conviction that the blessing asked for is being given and will declare itself in the future. This, seems to be an example of the unitive stage of the Christian life.

Conclusions

When they were baptised in the Spirit, the two figures we have examined became role models for the renewing work of the Holy Spirit in our times. Firstly, the experience of new life in the Spirit led them to question some of the theological and scriptural assumptions of the day, e.g. the charisms were given to the early church in order to get it established, whereas, now they are only given to a small few as evidence of rare sanctity. Kuhlman and McNutt, as representative and pioneering Charismatics, began to formulate a new theology in the light of their pneumatic experience, one that is increasingly endorsed by the church. The gifts, ordinary and extraordinary, such as faith, healings and miracles can be widely distributed among the faithful. They are not the preserve of the saintly few.

Secondly, these writers have revisited the scriptures in the light of their charismatic experience. As a result, they have drawn attention to the gifts in 1 Cor 12:8-10 including the charism of faith. They confidently maintain that Jesus exercised this kind of faith himself and encouraged all those who believed in him to exercise the same gift. They also agree that St James had the charism in mind when he talked about the prayer of faith i.e. its role in healing and in nature miracles. The two we have examined appreciated the link between Spirit-filled proclamation of the gospel, and its Spirit-filled demonstration by means of the charism of faith and deeds of power.

Thirdly, implicit in the world view of these two believers, is a powerful critique of a rationalist and reductionist approach to reality. Due to the influence of the Enlightenment it has been widespread in society. Unfortunately it has also infected a good deal of thinking and practice within the church. It denies in a prejudiced way that supernatural events such as healings and miracles can and do occur. These two have shown in practice and stated in theory that rationalism is alien to true religion. In this sense they have indicated how the modern Charismatic Movement is prophetic, God's word of hope to a wounded church and a broken world.

CHAPTER NINE

Growing in Faith and Exercising Faith

In the course of this study we have examined the charism of faith from a number of interrelated points of view, scriptural, patristic, theological and experiential. A provisional definition was proposed in chapter three. Having taken into account the insights gleaned in the subsequent chapters a more comprehensive definition can now be suggested. It is followed by an analysis of ten constituent elements of the charism of faith.

> The charism of faith is a gratuitous as opposed to a sanctifying grace, which is granted to some by the Holy Spirit. Rooted in the gifts of wisdom and knowledge, it enables them in particular situations, to discern with trusting conviction, of a heartfelt and expectant kind, that in answer to a prayer of either petition or command, the unconditional mercy and love of God will be manifested through a deed of power such as an exorcism, healing or miracle. Such edifying epiphanies of salvation are anticipations, in the present, of the future transformation of all things in the Second Coming of Christ.

1) The charism of faith is a gratuitous as opposed to a sanctifying grace. As we have already seen, St Thomas makes this point in his treatment of the charisms listed in 1 Cor 12 in both the *Summa Theologiae* and the *Summa Contra Gentiles*. It is given, not for self-sanctification, but for the sanctification of others. It is not necessarily a sign of holiness.

2) Instead of focusing on the existence of God, this form of faith focuses on the saving *activity* of God in accordance with the divine nature and promises. It endorses the line of Geothe's Faust, – already quoted – 'In the beginning was the Word, and the Word was the *deed*.'

3) The gift is given to *some* by the Holy Spirit. This point is rooted in 1 Cor 12:7. Implicit in this verse is the assumption that the person has been 'baptised in the Spirit,' and has thereby been predisposed to receive the gifts mentioned by Paul in 1 Cor 12:8-10, including the charism of faith.

4) No one can presume to have the charism of faith in every demanding situation. It is given in *particular* situations. In spite of the fact that they performed many miracles, the first disciples could not heal everyone. For example, we are told that Paul lacked the ability to heal Epaphroditus (Phil 2:27), Timothy (1 Tim 5:23) or Trophimus (2 Tim 4:20). People discern when they can heal in an immediate and existential manner by means of the gifts of wisdom and knowledge, which reveal what the will of God is.

5) Implicit in point four are two notions of time: *chronos,* i.e. secular, un-redeemed time in which we experience our on-going problems of a 'chronic' nature, and *kairos,* i.e. the sacred, redeemed time of the Lord, in which we experience the manifestation of God's salvation and healing. When the gift of faith is given to a person, *chronos* invariably gives way to *kairos.*

6) Heartfelt faith is evoked by inspired knowledge rather than being directly willed. It is trust of a convinced and expectant kind, which is quietly and effortlessly certain about what is happening or is going to happen in the future. This inner certainty often involves an affective dimension. It is a question of *'orthokardia'* i.e. right heartedness, subjective conviction, in accord with the objective will and word of God.

7) We noted that trusting faith of the wishful kind prays in the hope that something may happen in the future in accord with God's will – known in a notional way – whereas expectant faith of a charismatic kind, offers either a prayer of petition (Mk 11:24) or command, (Mk 11:23) with the conviction that something *is* happening, or is beginning to happen in the present in accord with the inspirations and promises of God.

8) It is God who responds to the prayer of petition or command, and performs a deed of power, either by granting the petition perhaps in a remarkable way, e.g. converting a sinner, or by performing a deed of power such as an exorcism, healing or miracle.

9) Epiphanies of this kind manifest the loving kindness of God

in two edifying ways. Firstly, they demonstrate in deed what has been proclaimed in word. Secondly, those who exercise the charism of faith in their ministry, almost invariably relate in a compassionate way to needy people. That compassion not only prompts a heartfelt desire to see a deed of power occur – often of a therapeutic kind – it animates such deeds, when they do occur. The person who prays or ministers is closely united to the compassionate heart of the Lord, and 'has that mind which was in Christ Jesus' 1 Cor 2:16. This is also an important aspect of *orthokardia.*

10) According to Cyril of Jerusalem, deeds of power, of whatever kind, are forms of realised and final eschatology. They are fleeting but real anticipations firstly, of the victory of Jesus over Satan, sin, suffering and death, in his crucifixion, glorious resurrection and ascension into heaven. Secondly, they are intimations of the transformation of all things in the second coming of Christ. As Peter says, 'According to his promise we wait for new heavens and a new earth, in which righteousness dwells.' 2 Pt 3:13.

Ways of Growing in Faith

If the charism of faith is a gratuitous grace, as St Thomas Aquinas asserts, can one legitimately desire to receive and to exercise this wonderful charism? St Paul provides us with an emphatic and assuring answer when he says in 1 Cor 14:1, 'Pursue love, but *strive eagerly* for the spiritual gifts.' However, it is a psychological fact that by and large we can only desire what we already know. Therefore it is necessary to grow in an understanding of the charism of faith, firstly in the scriptures and then in tradition and the teaching of the church. Once the significance of the charism of faith is valued, it will successively become attractive, desirable and God willing, a fact of experience.

Paul's theology of the charisms, as was noted in chapter three, is conditioned by his thinking about the body of Christ. The Jesus of the gospels, is really and truly present, by his Spirit, in the members of the church (cf. Acts 9:4; 1 Cor 12:27; Eph 4:12). If different individuals have gifts, such as the charism of faith, the Christian community possesses them. It is not important which member has an individual gift, for if one member is blessed with a particular charism all the others have it. As Acts

4:32 says: 'Now the whole group of those who believed were of one heart and soul, and no one claimed private ownership of any possession, but *everything they owned was held in common.'* While this verse refers to material possessions, the general principle can be extended to include spiritual 'possessions', such as the charisms.

1) Growth in Justifying Faith can lead to Charismatic Faith

St Cyril of Jerusalem said, as far as it depends on you, cherish doctrinal faith, which leads you to God, *and you will receive the higher gift,* i.e. the charism of faith, which no effort of yours can reach, no powers of yours attain. A person is enabled to grow in the virtue of faith by confessing un-repented sin to God and believing that for those who are in Christ Jesus as a result of baptism and personal faith: 'there is now no condemnation' Rom 8:1. Justifying faith is also nourished by means of daily prayer and regular scripture reading. As a result one grows to have an ever deepening knowledge of Christ and the power of his resurrection at work in one's life (cf. Phil 3:8-12). This kind of faith relationship, gives rise to an increasing, and unimpeded, awareness that 'it is God who works in you, inspiring both the will and the deed' Phil 2:12. While the deeds Paul refers to normally involve a faithful and persevering following of Christ in the ordinary circumstances of one's everyday life, occasionally they may involve a manifestation of the power of God, e.g. in the form of a healing or miracle. What St Cyril is asserting is that there is continuity between one kind of faith and the other.

2) Baptism in the Spirit and the Charism of Faith

If it is correct to desire charismatic faith, what else can be done in order to receive this gift? The charisms mentioned in 1 Cor 12:8-10, including the charism of faith, are normally experienced as a result of what is variously known as the 'in-filling,' 'effusion,' 'release,' or 'baptism in the Holy Spirit.' In the gospels Jesus exercised the extraordinary charisms such as healing and miracle working after his baptism in the Jordan (Acts 10:38-39). The Apostles exercised the same charisms after they had been inundated by the Holy Spirit on Pentecost Sunday (Acts 2:1-12). It was the same for the early disciples. The men at Ephesus only spoke in tongues and prophesied after they had received the out pouring of the Holy Spirit when Paul laid hands and prayed for them (Acts 19:1-8).

As we saw earlier, St Thomas Aquinas maintained that people could experience a number of in-fillings of the Holy Spirit. As a result it *lives* in them in a new way in order that they might *do* new things, such as exercising charisms, e.g. those of faith or healing. Contemporary scholars George Montague, and Killian McDonnell have written: 'The energising power of the Holy Spirit, manifesting itself in a variety of charisms, is not religious fluff. Nor is it – as viewed by many today – an optional spirituality in the church such as, among Catholics, devotion to the Sacred Heart or the Stations of the Cross ... It is the spirituality of the church. By that account it is not – let it be said clearly – the property of the charismatic renewal.'[1] As we saw in chapter one, Baptism in the Spirit is an integral aspect of the sacraments of initiation and normative for all Christians. Anyone who has experienced the in-filling of the Spirit is more likely to be granted the charism of faith.

If you wish to receive this grace you might find the following acronym helpful. DARE to ask for this blessing.

Desire to be baptised with the Spirit. Besides inspiring you by the good example of Spirit filled Christians, the Lord will allow you to experience considerable suffering, failure and even serious sin in order to evoke in you a heartfelt desire for the Holy Spirit.

Accept the scriptural promises to do with the sending of the Spirit. For example, Jn 7:37 says: 'Jesus stood and said in a loud voice, "If anyone is thirsty, let him come to me and drink. Whoever believes in me, as the Scripture has said, streams of living water will flow from within him." By this he meant the Spirit, whom those who believed in him were later to receive.'

Request God for this gift. Say the following prayer or something like it. 'Lord Jesus, I am willing to renounce anything in my life that might grieve your Holy Spirit within me. I want to be freed from sin and from all illusions and false inspirations. With your help I will turn away from all wrongdoing and I will avoid anything that might lead me to wrongdoing. I ask you to forgive all the sins that I have committed. I offer you my life and

I promise to serve you as my Lord. I ask you to baptise me in the Holy Spirit and to give me whatever spiritual gifts you wish me to have. I thank you that my prayer is even now being answered, through Christ our Lord. Amen.'

Expect to be blessed by the Spirit. The Spirit can come in one of the following ways, gradually in almost imperceptible steps, suddenly and dramatically, or after a delay of days or weeks. One knows that the Spirit has come by its effects, a closer more intimate relationship with Christ, great joy, a newfound love of scripture, prayer and people, etc.

3) Hearing the Rhema word of God

As far as I'm aware, there is only one place in the New Testament where we are told how to grow in faith. In Rom 10:17 Paul says: 'faith comes from hearing the message, and the message is heard through the word of Christ.' In the Old Testament the term for word is *Dabar*. It can be used as a noun and as a verb. As a noun it is objective. It refers to the word of God which is true in itself. The bible contains that word between its covers. As a verb it is subjective. It refers to the word of God which is true for the individual. It is the revelatory word of God which is spoken by God to a particular person, in specific circumstances. When the Old Testament was translated into Greek, the translators acknowledged this distinction. When the text referred to the word in itself, they used the Greek term *logos*. When the text referred to the word that is spoken, it used the Greek term *rhema*. When devout people pay attention to the scriptures they desire that God's word would leap alive off the page into their hearts as an inspired and inspiring word of revelation. The Lord describes this dynamic process in Is 48:6-8: 'From now on I will tell you of new things, of hidden things unknown to you. They are created now, and not long ago; you have not heard of them before today. So you cannot say, "Yes, I knew of them." You have neither heard nor understood; from of old your ear has not been open.' Derek Prince says that the relationship between *logos* and *rhema* can be expressed in the following statements: '*Rhema* takes the eternal *logos* and injects it into time. *Rhema* takes the heavenly *logos* and brings it down to earth. *Rhema* takes the general *logos* and makes it specific. *Rhema* takes a portion of the total *logos* and presents it in the form that a man can assimilate.'[2]

There are many examples of the power of the *rhema* word in the bible. For instance, when the angel Gabriel told Mary that she was to become the mother of the redeemer he said: 'for nothing will be impossible with God' Lk 1:37. Nothing in the Greek can be literally translated as 'every *rhema* word from God contains the power of its own fulfillment.' In the light of this assurance Mary replied, 'here am I, the servant of the Lord; let it be with me according to your (*rhema*) word.' Faith will be evoked in us when we like Mary we hear the *rhema* word of God in the circumstances of daily life.

That is why scriptural prayer is necessary. As Prov 4:20-22 says: 'My son, pay attention to what I say; listen closely to my words. Do not let them out of your sight, keep them within your heart; for they are life to those who find them and health to a man's whole body.' By using a method like the Benedictine *Lectio Divina,* we can listen to God's word to us within the particular circumstances of daily life. It involves five main stages, of reading a scripture passage, meditating on it, praying, contemplating the God who is revealed through it, and responding appropriately to the Lord in prayerful and practical ways. As a result of prayer times like these, our hearts will burn within us as God's *logos* word leaps alive with relevant meaning into the heart, to become God's *rhema* word. There it will often evoke unhesitating faith while empowering the hearer to do what God has promised, even to the point of healings and miracles. As the Lord promises, e.g. in Is 55:1, God's word always contains within itself the power of its own fulfillment.

4) The Example of Men and Women of Faith

Another way of growing in charismatic faith is to become associated, directly or indirectly, with people who exercise this gift. Many people have testified to the fact that their growth in charismatic faith was greatly helped when they attended a healing service conducted by the late Kathryn Kuhlman. For example, Steve Clark says that he saw many people being cured, especially a woman who had come to the 'miracle service' in the 7,000 seater Shrine Auditorium in Los Angeles. Before her healing she had to wear braces all over her body and walk with the aid of crutches.[3] Not all of us have had the opportunity of witnessing the ministry of such gifted Charismatics as Kathryn. But we can read about their lives and study their writings. For example, many people have found that inspiring biographies and books of testimony to do with Kathryn Kuhlman's life and ministry can help to nurture charismatic faith.[4]

5) Acting in Faith

The late Agnes Sanford author of the well-known book *The Healing Light*, believed that charismatic faith can be nurtured by acting in faith.[5] Briefly put this involves two main points.

Firstly, all of us are called to trust in the providence and the help of the Lord in our daily lives. Charismatic faith, as we have noted is trusting faith suffused with a God given certitude and expectancy. As we humbly acknowledge our weakness, inner poverty and absolute dependency on God, we will occasionally find that our trusting faith has grown into expectant faith of the charismatic kind. We will also notice that this kind of deep trust in God can be threatened by all kinds of negative states such as pride, doubt, fear, unresolved guilt feelings, etc. Therefore discernment of spirits is necessary. When we recognise such inward states – which may be prompted by the outer circumstances of our lives – we acknowledge that wherever they come from, from our own human nature or the evil one, they do not come from God. As such they shouldn't be allowed to compromise our trust in God. As the Lord promises in Is 41:10: 'Fear not, I am with you, do not be dismayed, for I am your God, I will strengthen you, I will help you, I will uphold you with my victorious right hand.'

Secondly, Agnes Sanford encouraged people to accept small faith challenges. In *the Healing Light* she proposed the following prayer exercise.

A) Lay aside your worries. Quieten your mind and concentrate on the presence of God.
Remind yourself that there is a source of life beyond your own.

B) Get in touch with that Source of life by saying a prayer like this: 'Lord of life, increase in me at this time your life-giving power.'

C) Believe and affirm that the power is coming into your deepest self. Recall what Jesus promised: and in Lk 11:13, 'If you then, though you are evil, know how to give good gifts to your children, how much more will your Father in heaven give the Holy Spirit to those who ask him!' Accept God's power with confident trust. It becomes yours as you accept it with thanksgiving. You could say: 'Thank you that you life is coming into me even now and filling me, body, mind and spirit.'

D) Observe the operations of God's life in yours. In order to do so decide on some tangible thing that you wish to be accomplished by that power so that you will know without question that your experiment succeeded, e.g. praying that a cold would be cured, that a relative would get a job, etc. Here is a personal example of what I mean when I say that we have to put our faith into action.

A year and a half ago I flew to Milan, en route to Trent, in Northern Italy. When I arrived – hours later than expected – the people who had come to collect me, had already gone home. Because I had no contact numbers, I rang my community in Dublin to ask if any Italian had been in touch. They said no. Fortunately, I had a good deal of money with me. So I went to a *bureau de change* and changed it into liras. Then I called a taxi and went to a cheap motel. The next morning I rang Dublin again. The Italians still hadn't made contact. I said that if they did, to tell them that I intended travelling to my destination by train. Then I took a taxi to the impressive railway station in the centre of Milan and headed North.

When I got to Trent I decided to take a taxi to the only address I had, a retreat center where I had stayed during a previous visit. When I arrived, I paid the taxi man and he drove off. Then I climbed the steps to the entrance and rang the bell. There was no answer. When I eventually noticed that the shutters were closed, it became evident that the retreat house was closed and deserted. I was in a quandary. What could I do now, where could I go?

I saw a house nearby. I walked over and rang the bell. A woman looked out of an upstairs window and asked what I wanted. I don't speak Italian, but using the few Italian words I had picked up, I tried to explain that I was a priest. Eventually, she nervously opened the door and let me in. I asked if I could phone a local priest. She agreed. I rang him, only to hear a message on his answering machine, which seemed to say, that he was away for three days. I was running out of options. I asked the woman if I could phone for another taxi. Again she agreed. A few minutes later it arrived, and I headed off to the priest's house. I hoped that he had a housekeeper who might return later in the afternoon. When I rang the bell there was no reply.

I walked off, pulling my luggage on a trolley. I returned sometime later, but there was still no response. By now I was getting disheartened. I had no money, no phone numbers, no addresses, I didn't speak the language and I was very tired, hot and thirsty. Finally, I stopped on the pavement. I had to acknowledge that I was powerless to help myself. I said to God, 'Lord, I am your servant. I'm here in Trent to evangelise. I'm trying to do your will. I know that in your providence you have a plan for me, and that you care for me. You have told us not to worry about food, drink and shelter and to trust in your promises. I cast my anxieties upon you and ask you to provide for me in these difficult circumstances. There is nothing more that I can do for myself. Quite frankly, from a rational point of view I can't see how you could help me. But nevertheless I rely on you completely, and praise you in these trying circumstances.' Then I headed off again, dragging my luggage behind me.

About two minutes later I was startled when I heard a woman shouting, 'Padre Collins, Padre Collins.' I looked across the road and saw a woman waving at me. She began to run in my direction. She was followed by a man who had just got out of a car. It turned out that the woman, a doctor's wife could speak quite good English. Evidently, one of my Italian contacts had finally, phoned Dublin. Giovanne explained that she had heard on the grapevine that I was coming to Trent. She and her friend had decided to look for me. Trent is a big town. Neither Giovanne or Flavio knew what I looked like. I wasn't wearing my clerical clothes that day. But they had prayed to God for guidance, and drove to the very street where I happened to be walking. When they saw a middle-aged man pulling a bag on a trolley they suspected that I might be the priest they were looking for. With a great sense of relief, I told them who I was. Then we drove to Flavio's home where his artist wife, Maria Lina, prepared a lovely meal, while I took a shower and consumed litres of water.

Through the providence of God and their extraordinary hospitality I had moved from being homeless to having a beautiful home in Italy! That was an episode I will never forget, one that moved me from problems to praise. Minutes after praying to the Lord in my powerlessness, he had used two of his faithful servants to be his answer to my heartfelt petition.

Exercising the Charism of Faith

The charism of faith is mysterious. Over the years, however, I have learned a little about its nature and exercise. There seem to be a number of discernible points in the dynamic of this special type of trust, namely sincere, wholesome desire; an inspired knowledge of God's will; and at least a mustard seed of expectant, unhesitating faith.

A) Sincere Wholesome Desires

The charism of faith is rooted in a God prompted desire for God's help. Such desires are sometimes known as 'holy desires.' When Jesus was ministering, he responded in a positive way when he discerned that people's desires were wholesome and prompted by the Spirit. For example when two young men said that they wanted to see where he lived (Jn 1:38), Jesus discerned that their desire was a Godly one. Genuine desires are usually motivated by such things as a longing for deeper relationship with God, and 'indignant compassion'. In other words, in the light of a loving recognition of the innermost value of a person who is suffering, a benevolent person angrily resists anything that might militate against the other person's worth and welfare. This gives rise to an ardent desire to alleviate his or her suffering. It is evident that the ministry of Jesus was motivated by this kind of love. When a leper in Mk 1:40, said to him, 'If you want to, you can heal me,' Jesus was filled with indignant compassion and replied: 'Of course I want to, be healed.'

But Jesus also recognised that many of our apparently good

desires are self-centered. For example, in Mt 20:21 a mother wanted promotion for her two sons. Jesus did not satisfy her desire because he discerned that it came merely form her ambitious human spirit and not from God. Over the years I have come to recognise that apparently benevolent desires, e.g. for the healing of others, can be unconsciously influenced by other more self-centered ones. For instance, when a person's faith is weak, he or she may anxiously strive to have it strengthened by signs and wonders as proof that God exists and that God's word is true. Spiritual pride and conceit can also be involved. The fact that a person believes in deeds of power can prompt a desire to perform them as a confirmation of his or her spiritual superiority.

B) An Inspired Knowledge of God's Will

If a desire is sincere and wholesome, one has to discern whether it is in accord with the will and purposes of God or not. In my experience this has to be done in a real as opposed to a notional way. While it is true that the Lord promises to answer prayer, and to heal the sick, that doesn't necessarily mean that it is God's will that a sick relative is going to be healed. One needs to be guided by the Spirit, in order to discern in an existential way, whether it is God's will at this time, in this particular situation. We saw in chapter three, how the gifts of wisdom and knowledge can enable a Christian to have an experiential sense of what God wants to do. Not surprisingly, scripture and the saints are familiar with this kind of guidance.

In Rom 12:2 we read: 'Do not conform any longer to the pattern of this world, but be transformed by the renewing of your mind. Then you will be able to test and approve what God's will is – his good, pleasing and perfect will.' The notion of a transformed life leading to supernatural knowledge of God's will is reiterated in Col 3:10, 'the new nature is being renewed in knowledge.' This is made possible by the Holy Spirit active within the human spirit. It searches everything, i.e. everything in the world and in the human heart. At the same time it searches even the hidden depths of God's divinity. As a result it can reveal God's intentions to the receptive mind. As St Paul says, it enables Christians to share in the mind of Christ and to be led by the Spirit (cf. 1 Cor 2:10-16).

St Vincent de Paul once wrote: 'Prayer is a conversation of the soul with God, a mutual communication in which God interiorly tells the soul what he wants it to do. St Ignatius of Loyola is well known for his rules for the discernment of spirits. They encapsulate the teaching of scripture and the Fathers and enable people to work out whether the impulses and desires they experience, e.g. during prayer, come from the Spirit of God, their own spirit, or the evil spirit.'[6] Commenting on Ignatius's theology, Hugo Rahner says that only those who have made a fundamental option for Christ are able to engage in this kind of existential judgment: 'Only a man with "purified spiritual perception" can obtain an unerring grasp of the divine will by means of a sort of sublime "sense of smell' for divine things."'[7] In chapter seven we noted how Thomists refer to the instinctive ability to discern God's will as connatural knowledge. As Gerald Vann wrote: 'In the virtuous person there is engendered a connaturality which enables him or her, without the necessity of reasoning, to judge intuitively what is to be done in this or that case.'[8]

The kind of inspiration described by scripture and the saints can occur in charismatic and non-charismatic ways.

Firstly, for reasons I cannot understand, it sometimes happens in a particular case, e.g. ministering to a sick person, that one recognises that one's compassionate desire to alleviate his or her sufferings is a participation in the compassionate desire of Jesus himself. As a result of this sense of heartfelt identification with the subjective dispositions of the Lord, one has a sure sense that one is praying within the will of God. St Aelred of Rievaulx described what can be involved in these eloquent and moving terms. 'A person praying to Christ on behalf of another for the other person's sake, desiring to be heard by Christ, directs his or attention with love and longing to Christ; then it sometimes happens that quickly and imperceptibly the one love passes over into the other and coming as it were, into close contact with the sweetness of Christ himself, the one praying begins to taste his sweetness.'[9]

Secondly, in a situation of need one can be led to a relevant scripture text. Instead of being a noun that is objectively true on the page, it inexplicably becomes a relevant, here and now, verb that is spoken from the page into the spiritual heart. It evokes the subjective conviction that it is a declaration of the Lord's will for this situation.

Thirdly, one can receive a so-called 'word of knowledge', i.e. an intuitive awareness of what God wants to do. Bishop Pytches describes the gift in these words: 'This is the supernatural revelation of facts about a person or situation, which is not learned through the efforts of the natural mind, but is a fragment of knowledge freely given by God, disclosing the truth which the Spirit wishes to be made known concerning a particular person or situation.'[10] Such a word can come in different ways, e.g. as a word of intellectual awareness, or a mental picture which is sometimes referred to as a vision.

For example, recently I celebrated mass at a conference in Glasgow. When communion had been distributed, I paused, asked the Lord to guide me, and prayed briefly for healing. At one point I had a spontaneous, imageless sense that there was a person in the congregation who was suffering from a painful, rodent ulcer. I also had the impression that although the sufferer was worried that it might be cancerous, it was still benign. I asked if anyone was suffering from that particular ailment but no hand went up. For a moment I felt that what I had assumed to be an inspiration from God must have come from my own unconscious. Then I had a renewed feeling that I was being guided by the Spirit so I prayed in faith for whoever was suffering from the painful ulcer. I should observe, that once I'm subjectively convinced that I have discerned the Lord's will, I can pray with expectant faith.

The following day a woman approached me. She said she had an apology to make. She explained that she was the person with the rodent ulcer. It was painful, not yet cancerous and happened to be on her breast. As a result, she was too embarrassed to put up her hand. However, she explained that as soon as her problem was prayed for, she felt heat in her breast. It had lasted for hours. She was subjectively convinced that she was healed. Time will tell!

C) The Seed of Expectant Unhesitating Faith

Christians need to be sensitive to the fact that they can't psyche themselves, or others, in a Pelagian type way, into expectant faith. This God-given grace is evoked, not willed. In my experience when people know that their sincere desire is in accord with the will of God, that awareness enables them to move from trusting faith of the wishful, hesitant kind, into trusting faith of the expectant unhesitating kind. One can even give a score out of ten for the degree of conviction associated with such charismatic faith. Even a mustard seed of the genuine gift is enough to enable a prayer of petition or command to be heard.

Given that this book is being written during the hundredth anniversary of the death of St Thérèse of Lisieux, perhaps we could illustrate the three points by a revealing incident from her life. Incidentally, this incident also illustrates what was said in chapter five about 1 Jn 5:16-17. Thérèse says that from the age of four to fifteen she was moody, oversensitive and inclined to cry a lot. Then at midnight mass, on Christmas day 1886, she had a life changing religious experience. She called it her night of conversion and illumination. 'Charity had found its way into my heart,' she declares, 'calling on me to forget myself and simply do what God wanted of me.'[11] There is good reason to believe that Thérèse had in fact been baptised in the Holy Spirit. She says that as a result of this spiritual awakening: 'I felt a great desire to work for the conversion of sinners.'[12]

Soon afterwards that desire found a focus when she heard how a convicted murderer, called Pranzini was facing execution. Apparently he had murdered two women and a child in the course of a robbery. Thérèse read in the newspaper how he had spurned the help of a prison chaplain. She said: 'there was every reason to think that he would die impenitent.'[13] Thérèse prayed repeatedly on her own, and later with her sister Celine, for Pranzini's conversion. She makes it clear that she offered her petitions in the expectant faith that 'the abandoned wretch,' would eventually repent. Her firm faith was rooted in three convictions.

> Firstly, she had a heartfelt awareness of the love of God as a result of baptism in the Spirit and a Spirit prompted desire to pray for the conversion of sinners.
>
> Secondly, she realised that she was praying within the will of

> God because the Spirit had led her in a providential way to pray for Pranzini.
>
> Thirdly, that experiential awareness that her desire was an expression of God's desire evoked firm faith in her heart. Speaking about her expectant faith, Thérèse declared: 'In my heart, *I felt certain* we shouldn't be disappointed; but by way of encouragement in this practice of praying for sinners, I did ask for a sign. I told God I was sure he meant to pardon the unfortunate Pranzini, and I'd such confidence in our Lord's infinite mercy that I would cling to my belief even if Pranzini didn't go to confession and didn't make any gesture of repentance. Only I would like him to show some sign of repentance, just for my own satisfaction.'[14]

The day after Pranzini's execution, Thérèse read in the *La Croix* newspaper that just before he was guillotined, the condemned man had noticed that a priest was standing nearby with a crucifix.[15] He cried out, 'quick, hand me the crucifix' and kissed it three times. A few seconds later he was beheaded. Thérèse was comforted by the conviction that her prayers had finally been answered. As she testified, 'my prayer was answered, and to the letter.'[16]

Conclusion

St Cyril of Jerusalem variously referred to the Charism of faith as the 'higher gift' and the 'mother of miracles.' In this chapter we have offered a comprehensive definition of this graced ability, while suggesting some practical ways of acquiring and exercising it. We have stressed the fact that there is something mystical and elusive about the charism. It properly belongs to that point in the spiritual life where the illuminative stage merges into the unitive one. That point of intersection is experiential rather than notional. The following two chapters will examine the ways in which a proper understanding of the charism of faith has important implications for a proper understanding of sacramental anointing of the sick and effective evangelisation.

CHAPTER TEN

Faith and the Anointing of the Sick

This chapter focuses on the role of faith in the sacramental anointing of the sick. It asks, what kind of faith is involved, is it doctrinal or trusting? It begins with a foundational passage in Jm 5:13-16A: 'Is any one of you in trouble? He should pray. Is anyone happy? Let him sing songs of praise. Is any one of you sick? He should call the elders of the church to pray over him and anoint him with oil in the name of the Lord. And the prayer offered in faith will make the sick person well; the Lord will raise him up. If he has sinned, he will be forgiven. Therefore confess your sins to each other and pray for each other so that you may be healed.'

This text refers to three life situations and the ways in which Christians can respond to them. If someone is in trouble he or she should pray. Presumably James had petitionary prayer in mind. A suffering person would ask for either the ability to endure, or to experience some form of relief. On the other hand if someone is happy he or she should sing a hymn of praise. This could either be done in private or in a more public way, e.g. during a prayer meeting (cf. 1 Cor 14:15; Eph 5:19-20). The third situation he deals with is the way in which a sick person and the community should deal with illness.

Who does James have in mind when he talks about a sick person? The word in Greek *asthenein* implies physical weakness, tiredness, and sometimes moral frailty as well. James Leahy points out that the word is occasionally used for those who are near to death. So the sickness is a serious and potentially a life threatening one, rather than one of the more ordinary illnesses we all have to endure from time to time.[1] The sick person is encouraged to call for the elders. This suggests, that, he or she is confined to bed because of the illness, and unable to visit the community or its leaders for prayer. The word for elders in Greek is *presbyteroi*. It is a technical term which is used to refer, not necessarily to older members of the community but rather, to its official leaders.[2] Dibelius, Kugelman and Gusmer stress the fact that the sick were not sending for lay people with a charismatic gift of healing, but rather for office holders in the church.[3] Dibelius writes: 'If this passage were speaking about pneumatics in possession of a charisma, or spiritual gift, then it would be calling for the "charismatic" gift of healing, as it is mentioned in 1 Cor 12:9; 28; 30. But instead, the reference is to the elders of the church: they must be the bearers of the miraculous power by virtue of the fact that they are elders, for otherwise why would they be called upon and not others? ... Their healing power must be connected with their official character ... We have no knowledge of a development within the Jewish community which makes an office the vehicle of strong ecstatic – pneumatic powers.'[4]

A number of observations can be made about this significant quotation. Firstly, although charismatic ministries are different from the institutional offices, such as apostle, presbyter, and teacher, they are not mutually exclusive. An elder could have the charism of healing.[5] For example, although he was an apostle and a presbyter, Paul, exercised the charism of healing (cf. Acts 28:8-11). Thirdly, in this quotation, Dibelius seems to equate charismatic ministry exclusively with healing and miracle working. But a person could be graced with the charism of faith, e.g. when praying for wisdom or the conversion of a sinner (cf. Jm 1:5-9; 1 Jn 5:16-18), without having the charisms of healing or miracle working. Fourthly, as a Protestant scripture scholar, presumably Dibelius would not accept that this is a sacramental text. However, in spite of a lack of conclusive scriptural evidence, Catholics believe that it is. That in turn raises an interesting question, is it the sacrament, rather than the elders which is the bearer of the healing power? The answer would seem to be yes.

When the elders come to see the sick person, they are encouraged to do three interrelated things. They must anoint the sufferer; do so in the name of the Lord; and pray over him or her with faith. The practice of anointing was nothing new. In ancient culture anointings were used for cosmetic, gymnastic and religious purposes. It is thought that anointing with oil was already a practice employed by the Rabbis. The custom is also mentioned in the gospels. In Lk 10:34, the Good Samaritan poured oil and wine into the wounds of the injured man. In Mk 6:13, we are told that the disciples 'anointed many sick people and healed them.' So as Bo Riecke observed: 'James's instruction to anoint the sick with oil is rooted in traditional Jewish conceptions and has a point of contact with a suggestion of Jesus himself.'[6] There is nothing magical about the anointing. It is not the oil that has medicinal properties. It is an outward sign of what the Lord is doing inwardly, as he pours out his healing unction.

James says that the elders are to anoint the sick person, in the name of the Lord. There is nothing magical, either, about the invocation of the Holy Name. Only those who have experienced the liberating effects of faith in the unconditional mercy and love of God and live accordingly, can truly minister in union with Christ and in the power of his name. Finally, James says that the elders are to pray the prayer of faith over the sick person. Again the practice of praying for the sick was an Old Testament one. In Sir 38:9 we are told that people who are ill should pray for themselves, 'When you are ill, do not rebel, but pray to the Lord who will heal you.' The Talmud also recommends prayer for the sick: 'He who visits the sick should not merely sit on a bed or a chair, but he should wrap himself in a cloak and implore God to take pity on the sick person.'[7] James says that rather than merely praying *for* the sick person, the elders should pray *over* him or her. Indeed Origen (c. 185-254 A.D.) was so impressed by the need for a 'hands on approach' that he interpolated the words, 'lay hands' into the text of Jm 5:13-16.[8] James says that the prayer over the sick should be made with faith. Did he have the charism of faith, mentioned by Paul in 1 Cor 12:9, in mind? The fact that he goes on to cite the charismatic faith of Elijah 5:17-19, suggests that he had. Dibelius supports the belief that the prayer of faith mentioned in Jm 5:15 involves the charism of faith. He says that it: 'Corresponds to the charismatic faith with which we are familiar from the stories in the gospels, a faith which looks for an answer to prayer, even expects miracles.'[9]

It has already been suggested that the charism of faith does not necessarily have to be associated with the charisms of healing and miracle working. In this instance, it is linked with the official office of being an elder, which would later find institutional expression in the offices of bishop, priest and deacon. Is James saying that if ordained men, pray over the sick with charismatic faith, they can expect healing to occur? The answer would seem to be yes. In fact in James's epistle, the promise of healing is unqualified. This would have made sense in the earlier charismatic era. If a pneumatic with a charism of healing prayed with the charism of faith, he or she could confidently expect a healing to occur. But that same expectation seems to inform this text, although the charism of healing is no longer, necessarily, involved. James seems to be implying that if elders pray for the sick, in virtue of their *office*, and with *charismatic faith*, they too can confidently expect healing to occur. Dibelius writes: 'The promise of healing is stated totally without qualification; the possibility of failure is not mentioned. This is quite understandable as long as healing depended upon the possession of the charisma. For then any disappointment would perhaps be explained as resulting from the lack of the charisma in the first place, while such explanation was no longer applicable, once the miraculous healing power had become the property of the presbyters of the community.'[10]

James adds that the prayer of faith will 'save' the sick person and raise him up. The meaning of the verb *sozein* which is used here, is ambiguous. At the most literal level it means that the sick person will be healed. But in the New Testament, it also means that the sick person will be 'saved.' For example, in the gospels, Jesus often says, as he said to the haemorrhaging woman, 'Your faith has saved you' Lk 7:50.[11] In Jewish thinking sickness was ultimately due to sin, either the sin of Adam, or the person's own individual sin.[12] This point was graphically illustrated in the story of the cure of the paralytic in Mk 2:1-13, Jesus said to his critics before restoring the man to health. 'Which is easier, to say to the paralytic, "Your sins, are forgiven," or to say, "Rise, take up your pallet and walk?"' So in one way or another, physical and mental illness is due to spiritual disorder. Therefore, healing has to come to the whole person, to the spirit first, and then to mind and body. As St James promises, if the sick person has committed any sins[13] they will be forgiven. Once that root problem has been dealt with, he or she will be raised up in mind and body.'

The Charism of Faith and Sacramental anointing

Historically speaking Mk 6:13 and Jm 5:14-15 have become the basis of the sacrament of the anointing of the sick. Over the centuries the liturgy of the anointing has evolved in the Catholic Church. The story of this development is long and complicated.[14] One could generalise by saying that one central issue has predominated throughout, namely, what did James mean by the Greek word *sozien*. Was it physical *healing* or spiritual *salvation*? Whereas in the early church the primary emphasis was on healing of the person, including spiritual and physical healing, in later centuries that emphasis shifted to spiritual salvation. For example, when St Jerome (340-420 A.D.) translated the Bible into Latin, he used *salvo* meaning to 'save' to get across the meaning of *sozien* 'to heal' and *egeirein* 'to raise up.' Because his Vulgate version of the Bible became the official Western text, this misleading translation influenced the subsequent understanding of the sacrament of anointing.

For most of the first 800 years, – in spite of the Vulgate translation – it seems that the anointing of the sick was associated with physical as well as spiritual healing.[15] In the ninth century, however, the Carolingian reform shifted the emphasis from healing to preparation for death. The Schoolmen of the high Middle Ages developed this line of thinking. They stressed the fact the anointing of the sick could remit venial and mortal sins. For example, Thomas Aquinas said: 'Extreme Unction is a spiritual remedy, since it avails for the remission of sins, according to James 5:15. Therefore it is a sacrament ... Now the effect intended in the administration of the sacraments is the healing of the disease of sin.'[16]

The Council of Trent discussed the anointing of the sick at its fourteenth session in 1551. The bishops wanted to challenge the Lutheran and Calvinist assertion that the rite was not a sacrament. They endorsed the view of Peter Lombard, who said in 1151 that *Unctio Extrema* was one of seven sacraments. They said that it was instituted by Christ and announced by James. The

Conciliar decree stated: 'This anointing is to be administered to the sick, especially to those who are so dangerously ill that they may seem close to death.'[17] Not surprisingly, in the period from Trent until the Second Vatican Council, the anointing of the sick was seen mainly as a way of preparing people spiritually, who were in danger of death. Prayer for physical healing was largely ignored. As a result, those who desired to be healed had to resort to private prayer, relics of the saints, holy wells, or go on pilgrimage to shrines such as Lourdes, where healings were known to occur.

The pre-Vatican II understanding of the anointing of the sick was defective for a number of reasons. Firstly, it did not do justice to the meaning and intent of the text in James. Secondly, although the sacrament of anointing, can and, should bring spiritual comfort to dying people – especially through the forgiveness of their sins – it is also a sacrament of healing for mind and body. Thirdly, the scholastic and Tridentine emphasis on the so-called *ex opera operato* effect of the sacrament, stressed its objective efficacy but failed in practice, to stress the *opus operantis*, i.e. the subjective importance of faith, that of the recipient, and also the minister of the sacrament. Not surprisingly, it virtually ignored the role of *charismatic faith*. But as this chapter suggests the prayer of expectant as opposed to hesitant faith, is the key to the understanding of James's text.

Happily all this has begun to change in recent years. From a Catholic point of view there have been two main reasons. To begin with, a number of the decrees of the Second Vatican Council drew attention to the edifying role of the charisms, including those of faith and healing, in the life of the church.[18] It stated that grace could come not just through the sacraments and priestly ministry but also through the charisms which can be given to any baptised person, clerical or lay. Because there is no *ex opere operato* dimension to the charisms, the emphasis switches to the *opus operantis*, i.e. the subjective faith, either of the one who ministers, the one who receives the ministry, or both. Added to this point was the fact that the sacrament of anointing was revised at the second Vatican Council. Pope Paul described its intent in these words: 'We thought fit to modify the sacramental formula in such a way that in view of the words of

James, the effects of the sacrament might be fully experienced.'[19] Four main changes can be highlighted.

Firstly, the council fathers modified the scholastic and Tridentine understanding of the sacrament.[20] They stated that instead of being called 'Extreme Unction' as heretofore, the sacrament was to be referred to as the 'Anointing of the sick.' Consequently, it was to be administered to those who were seriously ill, and not just to those who were dying.[21]

Secondly, the essential form of the sacrament was changed. Instead of focusing attention exclusively on the forgiveness of sins and spiritual comfort, it also focused on the healing of the whole person, i.e. body and mind, as well as soul. 'Assistance from the Lord by the power of his Spirit is meant to lead the sick person to healing of the soul, but also of the body if such is God's will.'[22]

Thirdly, the Council fathers said that the sacrament should be administered in a communal setting where family, friends and neighbours would be able to support the sick person by their faith filled prayers. 'The sick,' they stated, 'should prepare themselves to receive it (the sacrament) with good dispositions, assisted by their pastor and the whole ecclesial community, which is invited to surround the sick in a special way through their prayers and fraternal attention.'[23] Surely the most important disposition of the recipient, is that of faith. Ideally it would be a faith that is informed with God given wisdom (*gnosis*) and expectant faith (*pistis*). It would know that God *is* going to 'save' and to 'raise up,' i.e. to comfort and to heal.

Fourthly, the Conciliar document stresses the importance of faith-filled prayer as one of the four main elements in the celebration of the sacrament . 'The celebration of the sacrament includes the following principal elements: the "priests of the Church" (Jm 5:14) – in silence – lay hands on the sick; *they pray over them in the faith of the Church* (Jm 5:15) – this is the epiclesis proper to this sacrament; they then anoint them with oil blessed, if possible, by the bishop.'[24] The phrase, 'faith of the Church' can have two layers of meaning. It can refer to the five effects of the sacrament, which were first described at Trent and which are summarised in the *Catechism of the Catholic Church.*[25] It can also refer to faith in God, God's greatness goodness love, etc., and the promises of God, especially those to do with God's willingness to answer prayer. It is this second point, in particular, that James had in mind when he spoke about the prayer of faith, i.e. charismatic faith. The people involved with the anointing, the priest, the person who is ill, and the community need trusting faith. But they need to be conscientious and pray within the 'measure of faith' they have received (Rom 12:3), either trusting faith of the hesitant kind, or trusting faith of the expectant kind (i.e. the charism of faith)

At the moment, Catholic priests conduct many services for the anointing of the sick, as well as individual anointings. Judging by the sermons they preach, many if not most of them, stress the fact that the sacrament can bring about spiritual healing, and help a person to accept suffering as a participation in the sufferings of Christ. What they often fail to stress, is the fact that the sacrament can and does bring about healing of mind and body. This kind of unbalanced teaching is probably due to the Thomistic notion of anointing as a spiritual blessing in extreme circumstances. But St James, clearly and unambiguously says, the prayer of faith, *will* heal the sick person. Homilists and catechists need to stress the fact that the anointing of the sick is sometimes intended to bring about not just spiritual, but also physical and mental healing, if and when, either the minister, the recipient or some other caring person/s is graced with the charism of unhesitating faith.

When the clergy renew their understanding of the anointing of the sick, they can expect, on some occasions, to be graced with the charism of faith. In virtue of that fact, they will also encourage many of those whom they anoint. The witness of their own strong faith, will sometimes evoke the same kind of faith in the hearts of the people they anoint. When this happens, the Christian community will see many of its members being healed in mind and body. As Jesus promised in Mk 16:17-18: 'And these signs will accompany those who believe … they will lay their hands on the sick, and they will recover.'

Lay Anointing with the Oil of Gladness

The contemporary Charismatic Movement uses a prayer from the Roman Pontifical to bless oil, usually olive oil, for use by lay people. These men and women, either anoint themselves or other people who are ill, with the sacramental. The oil is referred to as 'the oil of gladness' in order to distinguish it from the oil of chrism used in the sacrament of anointing. The title is scriptural, and can be traced back to Ps 45:7 which says, 'the Lord has anointed you with the oil of gladness,' which is also referred to in Is 61:3 and Heb 1:9. It is interesting to note that in his 'Catechetical Lectures,' St Cyril Of Jerusalem refers to the oil used in baptism as an 'oil of gladness.' He says: 'As Christ was anointed with an ideal oil of gladness, that is, with the Holy Spirit, who is called oil of gladness because he is the author of spiritual gladness, so you were anointed with ointment, having been made partakers and fellows of Christ ... This ointment is symbolically applied to your forehead and your other senses; while your body is anointed with the visible ointment, your soul is sanctified by the holy and life-giving Spirit.'[26]

The practice of lay anointing is rooted in Jm 5:13-16. As we have seen, the presbyteroi were official leaders but not necessarily bishops or priests. The practice of lay anointing was clearly, prevalent in the post New Testament Church. A number of the earliest Christian writers such as Serapion (c. 350), Pope Innocent (416), Caesarius of Arles (d. 543), Elgius of Noyon (d. 659), and Venerable Bede (+735) refer to it.[27] They have a number of characteristics in common. The olive oil was to be blessed by a bishop, usually during the eucharist. The prayer recalled the uses of oil in the scriptures, and invoked the power of the Holy Spirit upon it. The following words of the Venerable Bede refer to some of these points: And let them pray over him, anointing him, etc. In the Gospel we read that the Apostles also did this, and even now the custom of the church holds that the sick are to be anointed by the presbyters with consecrated oil, and to be healed by the accompanying prayer. Not only presbyters, but as Pope Innocent writes, 'all Christians as well may use this same oil for anointing, when their own needs or those of the family demand. However, this oil may be prepared only by bishops. For the saying, "with oil in the name of the Lord," means oil consecrated in the name of the Lord. At least it means that when they anoint the sick man, they ought to invoke over him the name of the Lord.'[28]

The blessed oil could be used by lay people, in accordance with Jm 5:13-16A, either to anoint themselves or other sick members of the community, in order that they might be healed. If they administered the oil with the prayer of faith, i.e. the charism of faith, the ailing man, woman or child would be saved and raised up. Nowadays any priest can bless the oil. The following prayer was written by Serapion and quoted by Pope Innocent to bishop Gubbio in 416 A.D: 'We invoke You, who has all power and might, Saviour of all, Father of our Lord and Saviour Jesus Christ, and we pray You to send down from the heavens a curative power upon this oil, … so that it may become a means, of removing "every disease and every sickness," of warding off every demon, of putting to flight every unclean spirit, of keeping at a distance every evil spirit, of banishing all fever, all chill, and all weariness; a means of grace and goodness and the remission of sins; a medicine of life and salvation, unto health and soundness of soul and body and spirit, unto perfect well-being.' Many lay people use the oil of gladness to bless family members, friends, neighbours and acquaintances. Happily many of them have reported that it has brought comfort and healing of mind and body.

CHAPTER ELEVEN

The Charism of Faith and Evangelisation

As followers of Christ, Christians are committed to the compassionate task of bringing the Good News to the people of our day. Not surprisingly we often discuss the nature of such evangelisation, together with the motives and means we have of carrying it out. However, our discussions are, frequently, frustrating and inconclusive because we don't seem to be clear about the term evangelisation itself. The problem is a semantic and theological one. We have failed to appreciate the fact that there are different types and models of evangelisation. This chapter has a number of aims. Firstly, it will briefly describe the different types and models of evangelisation, so that the reader can identify which form he or she primarily espouses while appreciating the fact that other people primarily adhere to different types and models. Secondly, it will suggest, on the basis of scriptural and theological criteria, that one model takes logical precedence over the others. Thirdly, it will indicate that the charism of faith exercised in the form of deeds of power plays an important role in the effectiveness of this model.

Models: their Nature and Purpose

The notion of models is borrowed from the world of science. They are ideal cases, organising images which give a particular emphasis, enabling one to notice and interpret certain salient aspects of experience. Among theologians, Avery Dulles has shown in a number of his writings[1] how they can be used with helpful results. Speaking about such models, Dulles says: 'In constructing types on the basis of the expressed views of individual theologians one is moving from the particular to the universal, from the concrete to the abstract, from the actual to the ideal. The type does not exactly correspond to the thought of the theologians whom it allegedly includes ... As an ideal case, the type may be called a model. That is to say, it is a relatively simple, artificially constructed case which is found to be useful and illuminating for dealing with realities that are more complex and differentiated.'[2]

Because theological models represent ideal types, an individual person or group would rarely conform exactly to any of them. However, they would belong, predominantly to one or other, while incorporating characteristics of the other models in their outlook. It is also important to stress, that models are descriptive rather than evaluative. All of them are valid, and have their own distinctive strengths and weaknesses. Ideally, models should be clear and precise.

Evangelisation and Evangelism

The words evangelisation, which is used mainly by Catholics, and evangelism, which is used mainly by Protestants, are both derived from the Greek term *evangelion,* which means 'good-news.' *Godspell* was an old English form, from which the word 'gospel' is derived.

The word evangelism is used by Protestants primarily in reference to verbal proclamation, i.e. preaching and teaching, which intend to win the world for Christ and to hasten his second coming. It aims to bring sinful individuals to commit their lives to Jesus Christ as their personal Lord and Saviour. For example, Billy Graham expresses this evangelical approach when he says: 'If you have never accepted Christ into your life, I invite you to do it right now before another minute passes. Simply tell God that you know you are a sinner, and you are sorry for your sins. Tell him that you believe that Jesus Christ died for you, and that you want to give him your life right now, to follow him as Lord for the rest of your life. "For God so loved the world, that he gave his only begotten Son, that whoever believes in him should not perish, but have eternal life" Jn 3:16.'[3] Evangelical Protestants pray that evangelism will lead to *revival,* i.e. a sudden and dramatic intervention by God, that will bring about mass conversions similar to those that took place during the Great Awakening in New England 1740-1743.

Catholics have a wider notion of evangelisation. Pope Paul

VI expressed its aim in *Evangelii Nuntiandi* (18) 'if it had to be expressed in one sentence the best way of stating it would be to say that the Church evangelises when she seeks to convert, solely through the Divine Power of the Message she proclaims, both the personal and collective consciences of people, the activities in which they engage, and the lives and the concrete milieux which are theirs.' Whereas the Protestant notion of evangelisation has a clear personal aim, the Catholic notion is wider in scope, and therefore harder to pin-down. Catholics pray that evangelisation will lead to a gradual renewal of individuals and society as a graced result of the transforming power of gospel truths and values.

Interrelated Types of Evangelisation

It is commonplace in writing on evangelisation to distinguish between,

Pre-evangelisation, i.e. preparing the ground, usually by means of such things as Christian witness, social analysis and learning the language with a view to the explicit proclamation of the gospel. However these initial activities are already an intimation of real evangelisation and inseparable from it.

Primary evangelisation, i.e. the early stages of evangelisation by means of proclamation and witness which aim to get the church properly established. Arguably there are four sequential steps involved in this process.

> *Proclamation* of the Kingdom by means of inspired preaching. Announcing God's reign, through the outpouring of his un-conditional and un-restricted mercy and love, especially upon those who are materially or spiritually poor.
>
> *Demonstration* of the coming of the Kingdom, either through deeds of merciful love and/or deeds of power such as healing and exorcism which are made possible by the charism of faith.
>
> *Repentance.* In the light of the proclamation/demonstration of the Kingdom, the evangelist invites people to turn away from their sin in order to accept the Kingdom in faith.

Discipleship. Telling those who have accepted Christ how they can become his disciples by willingly accepting to carry the yoke of the Christian ethic as the expression of heartfelt commitment to him.

Re-evangelisation i.e. helping sacramentalised Christians who have received the sacraments of initiation to commit, or re-commit themselves, to the good-news in nominally Christian communities/societies. Speaking about the distinction between primary and secondary evangelisation *Redemptoris Missio* (37) says: 'it seems wrong to make no distinction between a people that has never known Christ and a people that has known him and rejected him, but continues to live in a culture permeated to a large extent by Gospel principles. As far as the Faith is concerned these two situations are quite different.' Arguably it is easier to convert a person who is a non-Christian in Africa than a disillusioned ex-Catholic in Europe or America.[4]

Catechesis, i.e. literally, echoing the Christian teaching, building on the basics by means of planned systematic teaching, in order to bring about 'a living, explicit and active faith enlightened by instruction.'[5] It builds upon the foundation stone of discipleship which is laid by means of primary evangelisation.

Witness. 'The first means of evangelisation is the witness of an authentically Christian life ... in short the witness of sanctity.'[6] There are a number of ways of expressing our faith in Christ. We have to be for others what Christ has been for us, e.g. merciful, compassionate, loving, gentle, understanding, humble, etc. As St Peter said to Christian wives who were married to pagan husbands: 'if any of them do not believe the word, they may be won over *without words* by the behaviour of their wives,' specifically by the purity and reverence of their lives and 'the un-fading beauty of a gentle and quiet spirit' 1 Pt 3:1;2;4. As Cardinal Suhard once said: 'The great mark of a Christian is what no other characteristic can replace – namely the example of a life which can only be explained in terms of God.'

Testimony. This term is used by Pentecostals, Charismatics and Evangelicals in two senses. Firstly, it can refer to the reply given by a Christian who is asked about his or her faith or values. As 1 Pet 3:15 says: 'Always be prepared to give an answer to everyone who asks you to give the reason for the hope that you have. But do this with gentleness and respect.' Secondly, when a person tells his or her Christian story, e.g. about their conversion to Christ, or their baptism in the Spirit, it is known as giving a testimony.

Action for justice. There is a growing realisation in the contemporary church that there is no true evangelisation without action for justice. Pope Paul VI said in *Evangelii Nuntiandi* (9) that evangelisation consists among other things of 'liberation from everything that oppresses us but … .is above all liberation from sin and the Evil One.' As a result Christians have to alleviate poverty and also identify and remove its causes in the sinful and oppressive structures of society.

Deeds of Power. Pentecostals and Charismatics say that not only should Christians proclaim the Good News in different ways they should demonstrate its truth by the witness of the way in which they live, , they should also perform deeds of power such as healings and miracles, which are the Good News in action. The charism of faith is the gift that makes them possible. They point to the fact that groups who ignore this aspect of evangelisation not only neglect a vital element in the of New Testament evangelisation, they fail to gain new members while losing many of the members they already have.

Inculturation. This relatively modern notion refers to the fact that gospel truths and values have to be adapted, without compromise, to individual cultures so that they begin to permeate and transform their traditions, customs, laws, arts, philosophies, etc. The host cultures, for their part, begin to express their Christian identities in distinctive ways, e.g. in local forms of worship and organisation. To enable this reciprocal interaction to take place, is to evangelise.

Alone and together these interrelated activities are legitimate forms of evangelisation. However, for one reason or another, many Christians mistakenly associate the words evangelism or evangelisation with a few of these types, to the exclusion of the others. Arguably there are three models of evangelisation. They will be briefly and tentatively described in this section.

Hopefully they will prompt the type of discussion that will lead to the development of more accurate models in the future.

Didactic/sacramental Evangelisation.

This model of evangelisation is head centered. It aims at orthodoxy, i.e. mental assent to the doctrines revealed by God and taught in an authoritative way by the church. Advocates of this model, presuppose that Catholics are evangelised in the primary sense described above, as a result of receiving the sacraments of initiation and living in the Christian community. Consequently, they see evangelisation in mainly didactic or catechetical terms. The role of pastors, teachers, and those who conduct parish missions is to build upon the foundations already laid in a sacramental way. This is done directly by preaching and teaching the doctrinal and moral truths of faith, in order to ensure right belief and right action. This kind of instruction is usually objective and lacking in an experiential or personal dimension. For example, preachers and teachers who espouse this model, rarely witness in a personal way as to how these truths of faith have impinged upon their own lives. To do so would be considered a form of subjectivism and self-promotion. Of course faith as trust is included in this form of evangelisation by means of traditional forms of popular piety such as devotion to the Sacred Heart and The Divine Mercy, both of which stress the importance of trusting in Jesus. Faith as committed performance is also accommodated, e.g. by groups such as the Vincent de Paul Society and The Legion of Mary.

Vincent de Paul was the founder of the Congregation of the Mission in the 17th century. His approach to evangelisation was typical of the sacramental-didactic approach. He firmly believed that people could not be saved unless they were taught the central truths of faith and were reconciled to God and one another by means of a good general confession and mutual reconciliation. For example, In a letter to a fellow priest Francois du Coudray, he wrote: 'An eminent person, both in doctrine and piety told me the other day that he is of St Thomas' opinion that he who is ignorant of the Trinity and the Incarnation, and dies in that state, dies in a state of damnation. Now that touched me very much, and still touches me, so great is my fear of being damned myself for not having incessantly occupied myself with the instruction of the poor people'[7] In 1631 he wrote again to du Coudray who was negotiating with the authorities in Rome on the Congregation's behalf: 'You must make them understand that the poor people are being damned because they do not know those things necessary for salvation and because they are not going to confession.'[8]

Although the didactic model predominated in Vincent's approach to evangelisation, he also stressed the importance of the affective and effective dimensions of the missionary life. For example, he often spoke about the need for an attitude of trust. He said: 'We ought to have confidence in God that he will look after us since we know for certain that as long as we are grounded in that sort of love and trust we will always be under the protection of God in heaven.'[9] He repeatedly stated that love, whether affective or not, should find effective expression in concrete forms of action, e.g. 'If there were someone among you who thought of belonging to the Congregation of the Mission, just to evangelise the poor and not to help them, to provide for their spiritual needs but not their material ones, I answer that if we meet such people that we have to help them and get help for them in every way ... This is to evangelise them in word and *deed.*'[10]

It is probably true to say that this model of evangelisation still predominates in the church of today. The present Pope puts a lot of emphasis on the need for instruction in objective truth. This is clear in the systematic and objective approach of the *Catechism of the Catholic Church* and the equally objective approach to moral truth in the encyclical *Veritatis Splendor*. The Pope obviously feels that the modern experiential approach to religion with its distinctive models of evangelisation, is in danger of devolving into relativism and subjectivism, i.e. the so called *a la carte* approach to truth and morals. Not surprisingly many preachers and teachers endorse the Pope's point of view in their own approach to evangelisation.

This approach has obvious strengths.

- It is traditional and has worked well in the past.
- The fact that it stresses the importance of objective norms gives it a clear sense of focus and purpose.

- It does not presuppose that people have a developed sense of self-awareness and conscience and is therefore suitable for people who might not have much education, or emotional security. Mary Douglas has warned in her *Natural Symbols* that subjective types of religion that no longer put much emphasis on objective norms, rituals and symbols, can end up catering for a fairly sophisticated, middle class minority who emphasise the importance of inner states.[11]

It also has clear weaknesses.

- An approach that was developed in the classical era of essentialist spirituality is not well suited to the needs of the contemporary, existentialist era in which we live.
- This approach tends to favour sociological Catholicism rather than deep personal commitment to Christ, i.e. extrinsic as opposed to intrinsic faith.
- Research has clearly shown that a growing number of people want a more experiential approach to religion.
- The fact that people have been sacramentalised and instructed in Christian truth does not necessarily mean that they have been evangelised in a primary way. This is a point that is often made by Protestant observers.

Kerygmatic/charismatic evangelisation.

This model of evangelisation is heart centered. It aims at *orthokardia,* i.e. authentic Christian experience as firm trust in the 'length and breath, the height and depth of the love of Christ which surpasses understanding' Eph 3:18-19. Advocates of this approach do not presuppose that Christians who have received the sacraments of initiation are *ipso facto* evangelised in the primary sense. For example, bishop Flores of San Antonio, Texas, expressed this point of view in 1970 when he said that a number of the church's problems will not be solved by getting people to the sacraments but by basic evangelisation. He pointed out that many Catholics have never been effectively evangelised in this sense, i.e. brought to trust in Jesus as Saviour and Lord, but rather have been sacramentalised.[12] Sometime later Cardinal Pignedoli said at a Synod of bishops: 'One of the most serious problems today is that of the evangelisation of Christians, because if there are no Christians they cannot in fact give witness to others.'[13]

As a result of often falsely presuming that Catholics are evangelised in the primary sense, there can be a crisis of trusting faith in the church. Directly or indirectly, it effects head, heart and hands. The crisis of the head is due to the fact that many Christians fail to appreciate that there is a hierarchy of truth and that some doctrines – such as those contained in the kerygma – are more important than others. The crisis of the heart refers to the fact that many practicing and non-practicing Catholics have not had a personal experience either of salvation or the in-filling of the Spirit. The purpose of evangelisation, therefore, according to Evangelicals, Pentecostals and Charismatics is to bring people into such a heartfelt awareness, e.g. as a result of a conversion experience and/or 'baptism in the Spirit.' The crisis of the hands refers to Christian action, i.e. living out the spiritual and ethical implications of the the experience of the Good News in one's personal and community life.

John Wesley's conversion experience typifies what this model aims at. Following a moral fall, he was disillusioned. In his diary he tells us that he met a Moravian pastor who said: 'Do you know Jesus Christ?' I paused and said, 'I know that he is the Savior of the world.' 'True,' replied he, 'but do you know that he has saved you?' I answered, 'I hope he has died to save me.' He only added, 'Do you know yourself?' I said, 'I do,' but I fear they were vain words.' Wesley says that sometime later he had a conversion experience when his heart was strangely warmed as a result of hearing Luther's *Preface to Romans* being read at a meeting in Aldersgate Street, London. 'I felt I did trust in Christ, Christ alone for my salvation. And an assurance was given me that he had taken away my sins, even mine and saved me from the law of sin and death.'

Evangelicals and Charismatics believe that the kerygma must be proclaimed and backed up with personal testimony, i.e. how one has experienced its saving truth oneself. Life in the Spirit Seminars, Cursillo weekends and Alpha courses are good examples of this model of evangelisation. Evangelicals and Charismatics also believe that the truth of the kerygma should be demonstrated not only in the witness of a holy and joyful Christian life, but also by means of the charism of faith which enables healing, and miracles to occur.[14] As a result, those who are evangelised in this way can come into the same experience as the evangelisers, as a result of a personal religious awakening. Afterwards it is expressed in a changed way of living. This model of evangelisation maintains that after conversion/baptism in the Spirit, people need good teaching, which is inspirational as well as catechetical in nature, and geared to deepen and consolidate trusting faith.

This approach has a number of strengths

- It stresses the primary importance of faith as trust.
- It is very biblical.
- This form of evangelisation is personal, affective and therefore experiential. As such it is suited to the needs/expectations of the historical era in which we live. As Harvey Cox has written: 'The postmodern pilgrims are more attuned to a faith that helps them find the way through life here and now. There is something quite pragmatic about their religious search. Truths are not accepted because someone says they are true, no matter what that leader's religious authority may be, but because people find that they connect, they 'click' with their own everyday existence.'[15]
- It stresses the importance of personal witness in two senses. Firstly, people must practice what they preach. Secondly, they need to share their own personal experience of faith by giving their testimony i.e. telling the story of their own faith journey. This approach inspires and encourages other people in personal rather than abstract terms. It fits in with the notion that faith is caught, not taught.
- It provides a good and essential foundation for subsequent catechesis in faith and morals.
- Whereas didactic/sacramental evangelisation has produced disappointing results in the contemporary church, this approach has been successful in renewing faith and commitment.

This approach has certain weaknesses

- It can tend towards individualism, 'my salvation … my experience' thereby neglecting the community dimension.
- It can tend toward subjectivism, where people place more confidence in their own feelings, and experiences, e.g. visions, prophecies etc., than in the official teaching of the church, which can be ignored rather than rejected.
- It can underestimate the importance of the sacraments as means of grace.
- It is a narrow view of evangelisation which is in danger of overlooking the importance of the socio-cultural aspects of proclaiming the good-news such as action for justice, ecology, etc.

Political/Developmental Evangelisation.

This model of evangelisation is hands centered. It aims at orthopraxy. It shifts the emphasis away from assent or trust, and places it on gospel inspired activity, a hands on approach. It strives to liberate people and communities from all that oppress them such as personal and structural sin which are inextricably linked. For example, Nolan says in his *Jesus Before Christianity* that there is no doubt that Jesus had in mind: 'a politically structured society of people on earth. A kingdom is a thoroughly political notion … Nothing that Jesus ever said would lead one to think that he might use this term in a non-political sense.' Sobrino has written in his *Christology at the Crossroads*: 'Jesus does not advocate a love that is depoliticised, dehistoricised and destructuralised. He advocates a political love, a love that is situated in history and that has visible repercussions for human beings … Out of love for the poor, he took his stand with them; out of love for the rich he took his stand against them. In both cases, however he was interested in something more than retributive justice. He wanted renewal and re-creation.'[17] This model of evangelisation is pragmatic in orientation, relatively new, and owes a good deal to the liberation theology which has been created in third world countries, especially those in South America, afflicted, as they are, by socio-economic injustice. It has also been influenced by elements of Marxist thought and new insights in Catholic social teaching, e.g. Pope Paul VI's encyclical, *The Development of Peoples* (1967). Martyred Archbishop, Oscar Romero, of El Salvador, seemed to exemplify what was best in this model of evangelisation.

The notion of praxis is central. Committed solidarity with the poor helps one to understand the true meaning of the Good News. In this model, while the gospel is proclaimed by means of word or action, it is assumed that Christ is already with the poor, and that evangelisation is helping people to recognise and affirm their dignity as children of God. It also helps to liberate them from the evils that would be alien to their Christian identity. This liberation can take different forms.

> Firstly, it can be seen in structural terms, namely, that there are laws and institutional arrangements in society which are oppressive, evil, and alien to gospel values. These need to be identified by means of social analysis, challenged and changed. By showing compassion and love in these practical ways, not only do these evangelists witness to the Good News, they themselves are evangelised in the process. This is the indispensable hermeneutical key that enables them to unlock the spiritual riches of the scriptures.

> Secondly, in Western countries where there are large middle classes, oppression is seen more in psycho-spiritual terms, e.g. as inner hurts which may be due to physical, emotional or sexual abuse, by members of the family, or the wider community. Arguably these problems are not unrelated to the breakdown in social solidarity caused by the injustices and false worldly values that inevitably lead to the split between the 'haves' and 'have nots' in society. Mother Teresa refers to people who suffer in this way as the 'new poor,' hapless victims of a famine of love. Their psycho-spiritual problems need to be alleviated by means of practical and therapeutic action which is prompted by compassionate love. As a result, human development courses, counselling, and therapy can also be seen as an aspect of evangelisation. For example, if one looks at the programs that are offered by retreat and conference centers in Western countries, it is striking that many of them are to do with such things as personality tests, the

inner child, dreams, healing of memories, the shadow side of personality, self-esteem, stress management, addictions etc. Subjects like these are animated by a search for meaning, inner freedom and self-fulfillment, within a Christian frame of reference. They assume that wholeness is virtually synonymous with holiness. Clearly, this second understanding of developmental and largely apolitical evangelisation would not be included in the perspective of liberation theology.

Thirdly, as Paul points out in Rom 8:19-22, the good news is for all creation. But at the moment there is an ecological crisis as a result of the ruthless exploitation of the natural world and the consequent rise in levels of pollution and global warming. It could be argued that people like Teilhard de Chardin and Thomas Berry who draw attention to these problems, and those who try to alleviate them, e.g. devotees of Creation Spirituality and members of Greenpeace, are engaged in a form of evangelisation which often complements the therapeutic kind already mentioned.

While these forms of evangelisation have a trusting and didactic dimension, the main emphasis is on the Good News as liberating action. However, it must be admitted that therapeutic and ecological forms of liberation are problematic as far as this model is concerned.

This approach has a number of strengths
- It is relevant to the needs of our time.
- It is experiential and practical in orientation.
- It is motivated by important biblical themes, e.g. 'blessed are the poor' Lk 6:20, and 'as often as you do it to the least, you do it to me,' Mt 25:40, etc.
- Besides alleviating poverty, it also tackles its systemic causes.
- It interprets the healing ministry of Christ in a contemporary and holistic way.

This approach also has a number of weaknesses
- It can neglect the importance of personal commitment to Christ.
- It can end up being too humanistic, either politically or psy-

chologically, e.g. substituting self-fulfillment for self-transcendence. This form of evangelisation is in danger of being either Palagian, or syncretistic and gnostic like New Age spirituality.

- It can be overly reliant on secular ways of thinking, e.g. the Marxist critique, or the Psychologies of people like Jung, Rogers, Assagioli, etc.
- This model is new and hasn't been well tested.

Assessment

Which of these models of evangelisation is best suited to meet the needs of the times? We are living in a fast changing society where the center of gravity is shifting from the experience of religious authority to the authority of religious experience. As it does, being gives way to becoming and theory gives way to process. This shift has been confirmed by empirical research in many countries. For example, *The European Values Systems Reports* for Ireland in 1984 and 1994 have indicated that across the generations, regardless of class or education there has been a shift from firm, to less firm adherence to religious authority.[18] A recent MRBI poll in the *Irish Times* [19] indicated that when Irish respondents were asked whether they followed the teachings of the church or their own consciences when making serious moral decisions, 78% said they followed their consciences. As Karl Rahner accurately predicted many years ago: 'The spirituality of the future will not be supported, or at any rate will be much less supported sociologically by the Christian homogeneity of its situation; it will have to live much more clearly than hitherto out of a solitary, immediate experience of God and his Spirit in the individual.'[20] John Paul II seemed to endorse the fact, if not the trend, when he wrote: 'people today put more trust in ... experience than in doctrine.'[21]

Because the didactic/sacramental model of evangelisation is essentialist in an existentialist culture, it is not well adapted to the needs of the time. However the kerygmatic/charismatic and the political/developmental models of evangelisation are each in their own ways, pragmatic and experiential in orientation and therefore more attuned to the modern mind set. Which of them is to be favoured? It is arguable that there is a theological sequence in the types of evangelisation, all of which aim to evoke faith. Trust in God as a result of experiencing God's merciful love comes first. Secondly, comes faith as assent to the truths revealed by God. It should be the consequence of trust – as was the case in the New Testament Church – and not a substitute for it. Finally faith as trust and assent necessarily finds expression in action, which has a reciprocal effect on the way people trust God and give assent to his revealed truth. If this is so, the kerygmatic/charismatic model of evangelisation would be the logical choice. That being so it is worth taking a closer look at what this model has to offer.

Power Evangelisation

In recent years a number of Pentecostal/Charismatic leaders such as John Wimber[22] and Francis McNutt, have stressed the importance of 'power' evangelisation. They point to the fact that following his baptism at the Jordan, Jesus did two main things, he proclaimed the Good News of God's love to the poor, and he demonstrated that Good News in deeds of power such as healings, exorcisms and miracles. The signs and wonders performed by Jesus, were not a proof that what he said was true, rather they were the Good News in action. Not only that, Jesus instructed the apostles to do the same. Like him, they were to proclaim and demonstrate the coming of the Kingdom of God. For example in Lk 9:1-2 we read: 'And he called the twelve together and gave them power and authority over all demons and to cure diseases, and he sent them out to preach the kingdom of God and to heal.'

Before his ascension into heaven, the Lord commissioned the apostles to do the same in the post-resurrection era. In Mk 16:15-19 we read: 'He said to them, "Go into all the world and preach the good news to all creation. Whoever believes and is baptised will be saved, but whoever does not believe will be condemned. And these signs will accompany those who believe: In my name they will drive out demons; they will speak in new tongues; they will pick up snakes with their hands; and when they drink deadly poison, it will not hurt them at all; they will place their hands on sick people, and they will get well."' There is clear evidence in the Acts and especially the earlier epistles of Paul, that the apostles did carry out the Lord's instructions. They not only proclaimed the good news, they demonstrated it in deeds of power.[23] As Acts 2:43 testifies, 'Many wonders and signs were done through the apostles.'

While there is clear evidence that the charisms of power were exercised in the first two centuries, it is equally clear that a few centuries later they had all but faded away. Why this happened, is not entirely clear. There were a number of possible reasons. Firstly, there was what Durkheim referred to as the ritualisation of charism in the early church. Secondly, there was a struggle between the institutional and 'charismatic' wings of the Christianity. For example, the Montanists, who were charismatic, were finally condemned as heretics. As a result charisms and charismatics were suspect. Thirdly, in the Middle Ages, the Aristotelian rationalism adopted by St Thomas and others, was unsympathetic to the notion of pre-rational forms of religious experience such as healings.[24] This tendency was reinforced by the Enlightenment world view.

As a result, the charismatic dimension of Christian life was either misinterpreted or overlooked in favour of the doctrinal and ministerial authority of the institutional church. Priests and people expected the Spirit to be manifested by the witness of lives well lived, but not by charismatic activity. St Thomas taught that canonisable saints were normally the only exception to this general rule, before and after their deaths. He wrote: 'True miracles cannot be wrought save by the power of God, because God works them ... in proof of a person's holiness which God desires to propose as an example of virtue.'[25] There is something ironic about this point in view of the fact that St Thomas states elsewhere that the exercise of extraordinary charisms is the result of gratuitous rather than sanctifying graces, and is therefore not necessarily a sign of holiness.

Ideally, however, spreading the good news will not involve a choice between presence and power forms of evangelisation. It will aim to demonstrate the truth of the gospel proclamation, not just by the witness of transformed lives, charitable deeds and action for justice, but also by the performance of 'signs and wonders' such as healings and miracles, which depend on the charism of faith. As was noted in chapter one, this view seems to be in accord with the teaching of the Second Vatican Council. It could be added, in the light of the Pauline theology of ministry, that evangelists are more likely to receive the charism of faith than others. There is an on-going need in the contemporary church to identify and affirm those who are gifted with this important ministry.

It would seem that in 1979 Francis McNutt had the ministry of evangelisation in mind when he wrote in an article in *New Covenant* magazine: 'A gift of preaching is strengthened by other manifestations of the power of the Holy Spirit. St Paul states that in his sermons he did not depend on arguments that belonged to philosophy but on a 'demonstration of the Spirit and power' 1 Cor 2:4. St Thomas Aquinas, in his commentary on this passage, states that the preacher of the gospel should preach as Jesus did, confirming the message either through healings and miracles or by living such a holy life that can only be explained by the power of the Spirit. If I preach the power of Jesus Christ to save and redeem the whole person, people want to see that power made real. They want to see the saving, freeing power of Jesus when we pray that the spiritually sick be given the power to repent, and that the emotionally and physically sick be healed, and may be made better as a sign that the message of salvation and healing are true.'

Pope Paul VI seemed to endorse this point of view when he spoke at the official launch of Cardinal Suenens's influential book, *A New Pentecost?* In the course of his address he departed from his prepared text to say these spontaneous words: 'How wonderful it would be if the Lord would again pour out the charisms in increased abundance, in order to make the Church fruitful, beautiful and marvellous, and to enable it to win the attention and astonishment of the profane and secularised world.'[26] There is evidence, as we have seen in chapter one, which indicates that in recent years the charisms mentioned in 1 Cor 12:8-10 have indeed been given to men and women in all the Christian denominations. By and large, Pentecostals and Charismatic groups who exercise the charisms of power have been growing fast, while those who do not, have been in decline. And the key to the ministry of evangelisation and genuine deeds of power is the forgotten gift, the charism of faith.

Notes

PREFACE

1 *Tertio Millennio Adveniente* (London: Catholic Truth Society, 1994), par. 45.

2 For example, Keith Ward, *Divine Action* (London: Collins, 1990); Bede Griffiths, *A New Vision of Reality: Western Science, Eastern Mysticism and Christian Faith,* (London: Collins, 1989); Fritjof Capra, David Steindl-Rast, Thomas Matus, *Belonging to the Universe: New Thinking about God and Nature* (London: Penguin, 1992); Michael Talbot, *The Holographic Universe,* (New York: Harper Collins, 1991).

3 *One World: The Interaction of Science and Theology,* (London: SPCK, 1986), 75.

4 (Jan 1998), vol. 48, no. 1, pp. 31-41.

5 Cf. George Montague, 'Freezing the Fire: The Death of Relational Language' *America,* (March 13th 1993), vol. 168, No. 9.

CHAPTER 1

1 Quoted by Bernard Mc Ginn, *The Growth of Mysticism From Gregory the Great to the Twelfth Century,* vol. 2 of The Presence of God: A History of Western Christian Mysticism, (London: SCM, 1994), 339.

2 Peter Hocken, *The Glory and the Shame: Reflections on the 20th Century Outpouring of the Holy Spirit,* (Guildford, Surrey: Eagle, 1994), pp. 16-22.

3 cf. Arnold Bittlinger, *Gifts and Ministries* (London: Hodder & Stoughton, 1974).

4 *The Glory and the Shame,* 79.

5 *The Glory and the Shame,* 37-38.

6 See St Thomas in *Summa Theologiae,* II-II, Q178, A2.

7 *De Vera Religione* cap. 25, nn. 46, 47.

8 *Retractionum* I. 13. 7, in Migne, *Patrologiae Latinae 32* (1877), col. 604 f.

9 Quoted by Albert Vanhoye SJ in 'The Biblical Question of "Charisms" After Vatican Two,' ed. Latourelle, *Vatican II: Assessment and Perspectives,* vol. 1., (New York: Paulist Press, 1988), 442-444. cf. *Mystici Corporis Christi,* 17, AAS 35 (1943), 200.

10 Pope Paul VI, *Pope Paul VI and the Spirit,* ed. Edward O' Connor, (Notre Dame, Indiana: Ave Maria Press, 1978).

11 Kevin and Dorothy Ranaghan, *Catholic Pentecostals* (New Jersey: Paramus, 1969), 7.

12 *Catholic Pentecostals,* 20.

13 See Thomas Flynn, *The Charismatic Renewal and the Irish Experience,* (London: Hodder & Stoughton, 1974). For a Protestant perspective see, Cecil Kerr *The Way of Peace: Peace Amidst the Conflict of Northern Ireland,* (London: Hodder & Stoughton, 1990).

14 Harvey Cox quoting statistics compiled bv David Barrett, in *Fire From Heaven: The Rise of Pentecostal Spirituality and the Reshaping of Religion in the Twentieth Century,* (Reading, Mass: Addisson-Wesley Publishing Company, 1995), 14.

15 *The Glory and the Shame,* 72.

16 Liam Ryan, 'The Changing Face of Irish Values,' *Irish Attitudes and Values: The Irish Report of the European Values System Study,* (Dublin: Dominican Publications, 1984), 95-106. Its findings were confirmed ten years later in Hornsby-Smith and Whelan's update study, 'Religious and Moral Values,' *Values and Social Change in Ireland,* (Dublin: Gill & Macmillan, 1994), 44.

17 'Contemporary Spiritualities and the Spirit,' *The Christian Conspiracy,* (New York: Doubleday, 1973), 103-104.

18 *Fire From Heaven,* p. 306.

19 cf. 'Theological and Pastoral Orientations of the Catholic Charismatic Renewal,' Malines Document 1, in *Presence, Power, Praise,* vol 3, ed. McDonnell, (Collegeville, Minnesota: The Liturgical Press, 1980), 42

20 *Life in the Spirit: Pastoral Guidance on the Catholic Charismatic Renewal,* (Dublin: Veritas, 1993), 7.

21 'Theological and Pastoral Orientations of Charismatic Renewal,' Malines Document 1, 39.

22 *Christian Initiation and Baptism in the Holy Spirit: Evidence from the first Eight Centuries,* (Collegeville, Minnesota: The Liturgical Press, 1991), 333.

23 'On Baptism' 20, quoted by J. Quasten, *Patrology: The Anti-Nicene Literature after Irenaeus,* Vol. 2, (Westminster, Maryland: The Newman Press, 1953), 330.

24 *Christian Initiation and Baptism in the Holy Spirit,* 337.

25 Silver jubilee edition of *Goodnews,* 1992, pp. 51-53.

26 cf. Evelyn Underhill, *Mystics of the Church,* (Cambridge: James Clarke, 1975), 9-10.

27 *The Practice of Faith: A Handbook of Contemporary Spirituality,* (London: SCM Press, 1985), 22.

28 (New York: Pueblo, 1984), 320-327.

29 David Pytches, *Come Holy Spirit: Learning How to Minister Power* (London: Hodder and Stoughton, 1985), 109.

30 D. A. Carson *Showing the Spirit: A Theological Exposition of 1 Corinthians 12-14* , (Carlisle: Paternoster Press, 1995).

31 (Collegeville: Liturgical Press, 1990).
32 *Crossing the Threshold of Hope,* (London: Jonathan Cape, 1994), 53.
33 'Jesus' in *The New Jerome Biblical Commentary,* (78:20), 1321.
34 Raymond E. Brown and Sandra Schneiders on 'Hermeneutics,' in the *NJBC* (New Jersey: Prentice Hall, 1990), ch 71, sec. 9, p. 1148.
35 Edward Schillebeeckx 'The Authority of New Experiences and The Authority of the New Testament,' *Christ: The Christian Experience in the Modern World* (London: SCM Press Ltd., 1980), 27-64.
36 Donal Dorr, *Remove the Heart of Stone: Charismatic Renewal and the Experience of Grace,* (Dublin: Gill and Macmillan, 1978). Avery Dulles. *The Assurance of Things Hoped For: A Theology of Christian Faith* (New York: Oxford University Press, 1994), 216.
37 Homily, XXIX on 1 Cor, NFP 1st. Series 12:168.
38 *New Jerome Biblical Commentary,* ed. Brown, Fitzmyer, (London: Geoffrey Chapman, 1990), [49:59], 810.
39 *An Introduction to the New Testament,* (New York: Doubleday, 1997), 532.

CHAPTER 2

1 *Childhood and Society,* (New York: W. W. Norton, 1963), 250.
2 William Jurgens, ed., 'Catechical Lectures,' *The Faith of the Early Fathers* vol. 1, (Collegeville: Liturgical Press, 1970), 352.
3 'Directions to Hesychasts' in *Writings from the Philokalia on the Prayer of the Heart* (London: Faber & Faber, 1992), 183.
4 (New York: Harper & Row, 1961).
5 *Two Types of Faith,* (New York: Harper, 1961), 7.
6 *Two Types of Faith,* 8.
7 Par 150. (Dublin: Veritas, 1994), 37.
8 Denzinger, ed. Schonmetzer, 32nd Edition 1963, 3008.
9 Faust, 1, 1224.
10 Unger and White, *Nelson's Expository Dictionary of Old Testament Words,* (Nashville: Nelson, 1980), 24-27.
11 *Nelson's Expositary Dictionary of Old Testament Words,* 75-76.
12 *Nelson's Expository Dictionary of Old Testament Words,* 357.
13 *Riding the Wind,* (Ann Arbor: Word of Life, 1977), 56-57.
14 It is close in meaning to *peithomai*: 'to believe in, trust in, entrust oneself to.'
15 Xavier Leon-Dufour, 'Faith,' *Dictionary of the New Testament* (San Francisco: Harper & Row, 1980), 188-189, and Christopher D. Marshall, *Faith as a Theme in Mark's Narrative* (Cambridge: Cambridge University Press, 1994), 54-56.
16 *The Experience of God: An Invitation to do Theology* (Dublin: Veritas, 1981), 55.

17 D. H. Van Daalen, 'Faith According to Paul,' *The Expository Times*, LXXXVII, no. 3, (Dec. 1975), 188-189, and Christopher D. Marshall, *Faith as a Theme in Mark's Narrative* (Cambridge: Cambridge University Press, 1994), 54-56.

18. Rudolf Bultmann, 'Faith' in Gerhard Kittel and Gerhard Friedrich, *Theological Dictionary of the New Testament*, vol. 6, (Grand Rapids, Michigan: Wm. B. Eerdmans Publishing Co., 1968), 217.

19 *The Central Message of the New Testament* (London: SCM Press, 1965), 69-70.

20 See summary from C. H. Dodd, *Apostolic Preaching and its Development*, and *The Essential Nature of New Testament Preaching*.

21 For more on this see Derek Prince, *Faith to Live By* (Ann Arbor, Michigan: Servant Books, 1977), 44-48.

22 *Pray in the Spirit* (London: Victory Press, 1970), 50.

23 *Paul*, (London: SCM, 1975), p. 242, and also *TDNT* vol. 6, 220-222.

24 Clement of Alexandria, *Stromata* vol. 3, quoted by Avery Dulles SJ, *The Assurance of Things Hoped For*, 219.

CHAPTER 3

1 D. H. Van Daalen, 'Faith According to Paul,' *The Expository Times*, LXXXVII, no. 3, (Dec. 1975), 83-85.

2 *Jesus and the Spirit: A Study of the Religious and Charismatic Experiences of Jesus and the First Christians as Reflected in the New Testament* (London: SCM, 1975), 311.

3 'The Concept of Charism in St Paul' *Catholic Biblical Quarterly* (vol. 55, no. 1, Jan 1993), 79.

4 (*Schema* p. 47) quoted in 'The Charismatic Structure of the Church' *Concilium: The Church and Ecumenism* (New York: Paulist Press, 1965) vol. 4, 5.

5 *Paul: An Outline of his Theology*, (London: SCM, 1975), 442.

6 Die Wirkungen des Helingen Geistes, (Gottingen: 1888), 86, quoted by James Dunn in *Jesus and the Spirit* (London: SCM Press, 1978), 4.

7 Wisdom and knowledge are charisms in so far as they are graced abilities to articulate inspired insights in persuasive speech. See Dunn *Jesus and the Spirit*, 221; Carson *Showing the Spirit*, 38; Kistenmaker, *1 Corinthians*, 421.

8 *The Holy Spirit*, (New York: Paulist, 1976), 150.

9 See David C. Lewis, 'Signs and Wonders in Sheffield: A Social Anthropologist's Analysis of Words of Knowledge, Manifestations of the Spirit, and the Effectiveness of Divine Healing,' Appendix D, of Wimber's *Power Healing*, 252-273.

10 William F. Orr and James Arthur Walther *1 Corinthians* , The Anchor

Bible, (New York: Doubleday, 1976), 282; C. K. Barrett *A Commentary on the First Epistle to the Corinthians,* (London: Adam & Charles Black, 1971), 285-286; D. A. Carson *Showing the Spirit, 3-40;* George T. Montague *The Holy Spirit: Growth of a Biblical Tradition.* (New York: Paulist Press, 1976), 152-153; Hans Conzelman *1 Corinthians: A Commentary on the First Epistle to the Corinthians* (Philadelphia: Fortress Press, 1975), 209; Ridderbos *Paul,* 463-464; Arnold Bittlinger, *Gifts and Graces: A Commentary on 1 Corinthians 12-14,* (London: Hodder & Stoughton, 1967), 32-34.

11 *The Holy Spirit,* 152.

12 (Chicago: University of Chicago Press, 1957), 669.

13 Orr and Welther, *1 Corinthians* 282.

14 *Jesus and the Spirit,* 211.

15 *Theology of St Paul* , (London: Burns and Oates, 1945), 426.

16 *Paul,* 464.

17 Joseph Brosch, 56 & 50.

18 cf. Arnold Bittlinger *Gifts and Ministries* (London: Hodder & Stoughton, 1974).

19 Lenon-Dufour *Dictionary of the New Testament* (San Francisco: Harper & Row, 1980), 290.

20 2 Cor 8:7, p. 411; Rom 12:3;6, p. 211; Rom 14:22f., p. 223.

21 Victor Paul Furnish, *2 Corinthians* , The Anchor Bible, (New York: Doubleday, 1984), 403.

22 *Jesus and the Spirit,* 211.

23 *Jesus and the Spirit,* 211.

24 Joseph A. Fitzmyer, *Introduction and Commentary Romans,* The Anchor Bible, (New York: Doubleday, 1993), 646, writes: ...This is not the charismatic 'faith' of 1 Cor 13:2 (faith that moves mountains).

25 *Romans,* 647.

26 *The Holy Spirit,* 214.

27 *TDNT,* 6. 213.

CHAPTER 4

1 William Barclay *The Letters to the Phillipians, Colossians, and Thessalonians,* (Philadelphia: Westminster Press, 1975), 34-37.

2 *In The Redeeming Christ* (New York: Sheed & Ward, 1963), 5-6.

3 *Jesus and the Spirit: A Study of the Religious and Charismatic Experience of Jesus and the first Christians as Reflected in the New Testament* (London: SCM, 1975), 75.

4 R. Bultmann, 'The Primitive Christian Kerygma and the Historical Jesus,' *The Historical Jesus and the Kerygmatic Christ* (New York: Abingdon, 1964), 34.

5 Gerhard Ebeling, 'Jesus and Faith,' in *Word and Faith* (Philadelphia: Fortress, 1963), 201-46. James Mackey *Jesus the Man and the Myth* (New York: Paulist Press, 1979); R. B. Hays, *The Faith of Jesus Christ* (Chico: Scholars, 1983), 140-142, 157-176.
6 Dunn *Jesus and the Spirit*, 212.
7 *Christ at the Crossroads* (Maryknoll: Orbis, 1978), 108.
8 *The Faith of Jesus Christ in Early Christian Traditions* (Cambridge: Cambridge University Press, 1995), 65-127.
9 *Romans* Anchor Bible, 345-346.
10 *The Faith of Jesus Christ*, 124.
11 Harold W. Attridge, *The Epistle to the Hebrews* (Philadelphia: Fortress, 1989), 356.
12 *Catholic Biblical Quarterly*, 52 (1990), 270-291.
13 *The Faith of Jesus Christ*, 159.
14 Quoted by G. Sloyan, in *Jesus in Focus* (Mystic: Twenty Third Publications, 1983), 35-41.
15 Geza Vermes *Jesus the Jew*, (New York: Macmillan, 1973), 58-82. See also John Meier in *NJBC* (New Jersey: Prentice Hall, 1990), 1325.
16 *The Faith of Jesus Christ*, 27.
17 'The Portrayal of the Life of Faith in the Gospel of Mark,' *Interpretation* no. 32, (1978), 389, 396.
18 *Faith as a Theme in Mark's Narrative*, (Cambridge: Cambridge University Press, 1994), 114.
19 *Faith as a Theme*, 117-118.
20 *TDNT*, II, 302.
21 *New Testament Theology* (London: SCM, 1981), 166
22 *The Faith of Jesus Christ*, 38.
23 *Faith as a Theme*, 120.
24 *Faith as a Theme*, 229.
25 *The Faith of Jesus Christ*, 38.
26 *The Faith of Jesus Christ*, 41.
27 *The Faith of Jesus Christ*, 44.
28 *De Carne Christi* 11.6 [Sc 216/1.260] trans. ANCL 15.189.
29 *De Trinitatae* III. 26 [PL 10.95]; trans. NPNF II/9/70.
30 *Eun* VI.2 [PG 45.717] trans. NPNF/II 5.184.
31 *S T*, 3a. 7.3. See also Alexander of Hales, *S T*, 3, inq. 2, tract. 1, cap. 4. The same point was made by Peter Lombard, *Sentences* 3, dist. 26, cap. 4.
32 'The Faith of Jesus' *Theological Studies*, 53 (1992), 407-408.
33 *Jesus Christ in Modern Thought* (London: SCM Press Ltd., 1990), 354.
34 *Jesus God and Man*, (New York: Macmillan, 1967), 104.
35 Quoted by Raymond Brown in 'How Much Did Jesus Know?' in *Jesus God and Man*, (New York: Macmillan, 1967),102; and 'What

Can be Discerned about Jesus from his Words Concerning Issues Other than the Kingdom and Himself,' in *An Introduction to New Testament Christology* (London: Geoffrey Chapman, 1994), 28.

36 *The Assurance of Things Hoped For: A Theology of Christian Faith* (New York: Oxford University Press, 1994), 280; 150.

CHAPTER 5

1 *New Testament Theology* , (London: SCM, 1981), 165.

2 *New Testament Theology*, 35-36.

3 *On Religion: Speeches to its Cultural Despisers* (San Francisco: Harper & Row, 1958), 12.

4 *Jesus Before Christianity*, (London: DLT, 1992), 151-152.

5 *Catechism of the Catholic Church*, par. 302.

6 Rediscovering the Teaching of Jesus (London: SCM, 1967), 136.

7 C. S. Mann, The Anchor Bible vol. 27, *Mark* (New York: Doubleday, 1986), 282; Marshall *Faith as a Theme in Mark's Narrative* (Cambridge: Cambridge University Press, 1994), 101.

8 See Morton Kelsey, *Healing and Christianity* (London: SCM, 1973), 109-110.

9 *Dictionary of the New Testament* (San Francisco: Harper & Row, 1980), 316.

10 Martin Dibelius, *James* (Philadelphia: Fortress, 1976), 45.

11 The Anchor Bible, *Letter of James* (New York: Doubleday, 1994), 180.

12 *James*, 81, e.g. Mk 2:5; 4:20; 5:34, 36; 9:23f; Mt 8:10; 9:28.

13 *James*, 81.

14 *Letter of James*, 336.

15 Raymond E. Brown, The Anchor Bible, *The Epistles of John*, (New York: Doubleday, 1982), 35.

16 The Anchor Bible, *The Epistles of John* (New York: Doubleday, 1982), 615-617.

17 *Jerome Biblical Commentary* (New York: Prentice Hall, 1969).

18 *The Johannine Epistles* , 64.

19 'Conference X on Prayer' in *The Fire and the Cloud: An Anthology of Catholic Spirituality*, ed. David Flemming (London: Geoffrey Chapman, 1978), 35.

CHAPTER 6

1 *Faith in the Synoptic Gospels*, 'Pistis as Trust in God,' nos. 6 & 7, pp. 12-13; *Jesus and the Spirit, 74-76; Faith as a Theme in Mark's Narrative* (Cambridge: Cambridge University Press, 1994), 164-172; *The Faith of Jesus Christin Early Christian Traditions,* (Cambridge: Cambridge University Press, 1995), 24-64.

2 *Mark*: The Anchor Bible, (New York: Doubleday, 1986), 441; 452 *A Marginal Jew*, 888.

3 *Faith to Live By* (South Bend, Indiana: Servant, 1977), 28; *The Holy Spirit*, (New York: Paulist, 1976), 152.
4 *Faith as a Theme*, 169.
5 Jeremias *New Testament Theology* 161, Meier *A Marginal Jew II: Rethinking the Historical Jesus* (New York: Doubleday, 1994), 889. Marshall *Faith as a Theme*, 166.
6 *Faith as a Theme*, 169.
7 *Faith as a Theme*, 168.
8 E. D. O'Connor, *Faith in the Synoptic Gospels: A Problem in the Correlation of Scripture* (South Bend: University of Notre Dame Press, 1961), 14.
9 *Spiritual Exercises*, translated by Louis J. Puhl, (Chicago: Loyola University Press, 1951), par. 2.
10 John P. Meier, *Matthew: New Testament Message* 3, (Wilmington: Michael Grazier Inc., 1980), 194.
11 *Rediscovering the Teaching of Jesus*, (London: SCM Press, 1967), 141.
12 C. Hunzinger *TDNT*, (In one vol), (Grand Rapids, Mich: Eerdmans/Paternoster Press, 1985), 1028.
13 *Matthew: New Testament Message*, 89. See also Meier, *A Marginal Jew II*, 924-933.
14 J. L. McKenzie, 'The Gospel according to Matthew,' *JBC* (New Jersey: Prentice Hall, 1968), 43:59, 77.
15 Meier, *A Marginal Jew II*, 907.
16 *The Assurance of Things Hoped For*, 11.

CHAPTER 7

1 *First Apology*, lxi, ANF 1:183.
2 Quoted by Eusebius in *History*, 153-154.
3 *Nicene and Post-Nicene Fathers of the Christian Church* , vol. XII, ed. P. H. Schaff, (Grand Rapids: Wm. Eerdmans), 172.
4 *The Nicene and Post-Nicene Fathers of the Christian Church*, vol. X, ed. Philip Schaff, (Grand Rapids: Eerdmans, 1986), 355.
5 Homily 74, *Fathers of the Church* , vol. 41, trans. Sr Thomas Aquinas Goggin, (New York: Fathers of the Church Inc., 1960), 296-297.
6 *The Faith of the Early Fathers*, vol. 1, (Collegeville: Liturgical Press, 1970), 352-353.
7 151.
8 *Life of St Antony*, xlviii, NFP 2nd series 4:209.
9 *The Ancient Witness* (London: Associated University Presses), 198-199
10 *Early Christian Biographies* (Washington DC: The Catholic University Press of America, 1952), 378.
11 cf. Gerald Vann, *The Divine Pity: A Sudy in the Social Implications of the Beatitudes* (London: Fontana, 1967).

12 cf. Frank Sullivan, *Charisms and Charismatic Renewal* (Ann Arbor: Servant, 1982), 71.
13 *ST*, I Q. 43, A. 6, rep. Obj. 2.
14 *ST*, 1 Q. 43, A. 6, rep. Obj. 6.
15 *The Gifts of the Spirit*, (New York: New City Press, 1995), 27.
16 *ST*, I-II, A. 111, A5.
17 *ST*, I-II, Q111, A4; II-II, Q117, A1; *S CG*, trans. Vernon J. Bourke (New York: Image Books, 1956), ch. 154, pp. 239ff.
18 *Summa Theologiae: A Concise Translation* , ed. Mc Dermott, (London: Methuen, 1991), 370.
19 *ST*, II-II, Q. 45, A. 2-4.
20 *ST*, I, Q. 43, A. 5, rep. Obj. 2.
21 *ST*, I-II, Q.111, A.4.
22 *ST*, I-II, Q.111 A.4, Reply obj. 4.
23 *SCG*, Book 3, ch. 154, [4].
24 *ST*, I-II, Q. 111, A. 4, reply obj. 2.
25 *The Gifts of the Spirit* 32.
26 *ST*, II-II A.178, A.1.
27 *ST*, II-II Q.178, A.1.
28 *ST*, II-II Q178, A1.
29 *ST*, II-II, Q.178, A.1., Objection 5.
30 *ST*, II-II, Q.178, A. 1.
31 *Healing and Christianity*, (London: SCM, 1973), 218.

CHAPTER 8

1 Warner reveals in *Kathryn Kuhlman:The Woman Behind the Miracles* Ann Arbor, Michigan: Servant Publications, 1993), 104, that he eventually died in prison. He had been convicted of cheating a woman of money. He never paid alimony to his wife or visited his children or nine grandchildren.
2 Quoted in *Daughter of Destiny: Kathryn Kuhlman Her Story* (Plainfield, New Jersey: Logos International, 1978), 81.
3 Kathryn Kuhlman *I Believe in Miracles* (London: Lakeland, 1974), 196.
4 *Daughter of Destiny*, 93.
5 Orr's healing is recounted in chapter four of *I Believe in Miracles* 37-43.
6 *I Believe in Miracles*, 198.
7 John Wimber, *Power Healing* (London: Hodder & Stoughton, 1986), 176-199, & also Agnes Sanford, 'The Gift of Wisdom,' and 'The Gift of Knowledge' in *The Healing Gifts of the Spirit* (San Francisco: Harper & Row, 1984), 73-86; 107-124. David Pytches, 'Words of Knowledge,' *Come Holy Spirit* (London: Hodder & Stoughton, 1987), 99-108. Pat Collins, 'Words of Knowledge' in *Agape* vol. 5, no. 9, Sept. '86, pp. 12-15.

8 *I Believe in Miracles,* 199. Emilien Tardif *Jesus is the Messiah* (Melbourne: Manna Publications, 1991), 110-112; *Jesus is Alive* (Melbourne: Manna Publications, 1989), 39-46. Ralph A. DiOrio *A Miracle to Proclaim: Firsthand Experiences of Healing* (New York: Image, 1984), John Wimber *Power Healing* (London: Hodder and Stoughton, 1986).
9 In *Daughter of Destiny,* p. 126.
10 On 'The falling Phenomenon.' Pat Collins *Maturing in the Spirit* (Dublin: Columba, 1991), 149-155.
11 'Faith' in *I Believe in Miracles* 200-204, and 'Faith' *A Glimpse Into Glory* (New York: Logos, 1979), ch. 12, 43-49.
12 *A Glimpse into Glory,* 44.
13 *A Glimpse into Glory,* 45.
14 *I Believe in Miracles,* 202.
15 *A Glimpse into Glory,* 43 and *I Believe in Miracles,* 200.
16 *A Glimpse into Glory,* 45
17 *I Believe in Miracles,* (London: Lakeland, 1974), 203.
18 *I Believe in Miracles* 204.
19 *I Believe in Miracles,* 201-202.
20 *I Believe in Miracles,* 201.
21 *Daughter of Destiny,* 211.
22 Francis McNutt *Healing* (Notre Dame, Indiana: Ave Maria Press, 1974), 13.
23 *Healing,* 113-148.
24 *Healing,* 126.
25 *Healing,* 131; 139.
26 *Healing,* 120-121.
27 127-128.

CHAPTER 9

1 *Christian Initiation and Baptism in the Spirit* (Collegeville: Liturgical Press, 1991), 337.
2 *Faith to Live By* (Ann Arbor, Michigan: Servant, 1977), 83.
3 *Growing in Faith* (Notre Dame, Indiana: Charismatic Renewal Services, 1972), 15-17.
4 (Rockford: Tan, 1977) books such as *The Cross and the Switchblade,* the biographies of Kathryn Kuhlman by Buckingham and Warner, Kathryn's three books of testimonies, which have already been mentioned including *A Glimpse of Glory* and Simi and Sigreti, *St Francis of Paola God's Miracle Worker Supreme,* (Rockford, Illinois: Tan, 1977) can help one to understand and to desire the charism of faith.
5 (Evesham, Worcs: Arthur James Limited, 1974), 19.

6 Quoted by Hugo Rahner, *Ignatius the Theologian* (London: Geoffrey Chapman, 1990), 149.
7 *Ignatius the Theologian*, 170.
8 *St Thomas Aquinas* (London: Hague and Gill, 1940), 148.
9 St Aelred of Rievaulx *Spiritual Friendship* (Kalamazoo: Cistercian Publications, 1974), 131.
10 David Pytches, *Come Holy Spirit* (London: Hodder & Stoughton, 1985), 99.
11 *Autobiography of a Saint*, (London: Harvill Press, 1958), 128
12 *Autobiography*, 128
13 *Autobiography*, 129
14 *Autobiography*, 129
15 For the full text see Bernard Bro, *The Little Way: The Spirituality of Therese of Lisieux* (London: Darton, Longman & Todd, 1979), 69-70.
16 *Autobiography*, 129.

CHAPTER 10

1 James Leahy 'The Epistle of James,' *Jerome Biblical Commentary*, (New Jersey: Prentice Hall, 1968) [59:35], 376, where he refers to Jn 4:46-47; 11:1, 4, 14; Acts 9:37. Kugelman *James and Jude*, New Testament Message 19, (Wilmington: Michael Glazier, 1980), 63.
2 Dufour, 'Presbyter,' *Dictionary of the New Testament*, (San Francisco: Harper & Row, 1980), 334. See also Raymond Brown, 'Episcope and Episkopos: The New Testament Evidence,' *Theological Studies*, 41, (1980), 322-338.
3 Martin Dibelius, *James*, (Philadelphia: Fortress Press, 1976), 252; Kugelman *James and Jude*, 63-64; Charles W. Gusmer, *And You Visited Me: Sacramental Ministry to the Sick and the Dying*, (New York: Pueblo Publishing Company, 1984), 9.
4 James 252. *The Real Jesus* (San Francisco: Harper/Collins, 1997), 94,
5 G. Bornkamm in an article on 'Old. Elder' in *Theological Dictionary of the New Testament*, abridged in 1 vol., trans. & ed. Bromiley, (Grand Rapids: Wm Eerdmans, 1985), 933.
6 *The Epistles of James Peter and Jude*, The Anchor Bible, vVol. 37, (New York: Doubleday, 1964), 59.
7 Quoted by Kugelman *James & Jude*, 64.
8 *On Leviticus*, Homily 2.
9 *James*, 254.
10 *James*, 254.
11 For example, Mk 5:34; 10:52; Mt 9:22; Lk 7:50; 8:48; 17:19; 18:42.
12 The link between sin and sickness is made in a number of places, e.g. 1 Cor 11:29-30

13 McNutt says in *Healing*, (Notre Dame: Ave Maria Press, 1974), 279, that in the Greek, the word sins, probably refers to grave sins.

14 Gusmer provides a good overview in ch. 1, of *And You Visited Me*, (New York: Pueblo Publishing Company, 1984), 3-42. Francis McNutt, 'History of Anointing,' *Healing*, 279-285.

15 In 'Unction' in *The Oxford Dictionary of the Christian Church* 2nd. Edition, eds. Cross and Livingstone, (Oxford: Oxford University Press, 1983), 1406.

16 *Summa Theologica*, III-Supp. 29.1., quoted by Morton Kelsey, *Healing & Christianity* (London: SCM, 1973), 209.

17 'Extreme Unction' *The Canons and decrees of the Sacred and Ecumenical Council of Trent* trans. J. Waterworth, (London: Dolman, 1848), 105f.

18 *Constitution on the Church*, par. 12, *Constitution on the Laity*, par. 3.

19 Apostolic constitution *Sacram Unctionem Infirmorum* Nov. 30th. 1972. *Worship and Liturgy: Official Catholic Teachings*, ed. James Megivern, (Wilmington: Mc Grath Publishing Co., 1978), 425-428.

20 'Constitution on the Liturgy' par. 73. Vatican Council II: *The Conciliar and Post Conciliar Documents*, gen. ed., Austin Flannery, (Wilmington: Scholarly Resources, 1975), 1-56.

21 *Catechism of the Catholic Church* (Dublin: Veritas, 1984), par. 1514.

22 *Catechism*, par. 1520.

23 *Catechism*, par. 1516.

24 *Catechism*, par. 1519.

25 *Catechism* , par. 1532 lists 5,

26 J. Patout Burns SJ and G. M. Fagin SJ, *Message of the Fathers of the Church: The Holy Spirit* (Wilmington, Delaware: Michael Glazier, Inc., 1984), vol. 3., 97.

27 Gusmer, *And You Visited Me* 11-18.

28 Paul F. Palmer ed., *Sacraments and Forgiveness Sources of Christian Theology II*. (Westminster: Newman Press, 1959), 286-287.

CHAPTER 11

1 *Models of the Church* (New York: Doubleday, 1974); *Models of Revelation* (Dublin: Gill & Macmillan, 1983); 'The Meaning of Faith Considered in Relationship to Justice' The Faith that Does Justice ed. J. C. Haughey, (New York: Paulist Press, 1977); *The Assurance of Things Hoped For: A Theology of Christian Faith* (New York: Oxford University Press, 1994).

2 *Models of Revelation*, 30.

3 'The Holy Spirit and Salvation,' in *The Holy Spirit*, (London: Fount, 1980), 59-60.

4 On this see Aylward Shorter, 'Secularism and the New

Evangelization,' *Evangelization and Culture* (London: Geoffrey Chapman, 1994), 78-79.

5 *Christus Dominus*, (14).

6 *Evangelii Nuntiandi*, par. 42.

7 Quoted by Jacques Delarue, *The Missionary Ideal of the Priest According to St Vincent de Paul*, (Chicago: Vincentian Publications, 1993), 85.

8 Quoted by Luigi Mezzadri, *A Short Life of St. Vincent de Paul*, (Dublin: Columba, 1992), 31.

9 'Common Rules,' 11, 2, *Constitutions and Statutes of the Congregation of the Mission* (Philadelphia: Vincentian Publications, 1989), 108.

10 *Collected Works* XII, 87.

11 'To Inner Experience,' (London: Pelican, 1973), 40-58.

12 Ralph Martin, *Unless the Lord Build the House*, (Notre Dame: Ave Maria Press, 1971), 11.

13 Quoted by Ralph Martin from *L'Osservatore Romano* in *Fire on the Earth*, (Ann Arbor, Mich: Word of Life, 1975), 13.

14 See, John Wimber, 'Power versus Programme', *Power Evangelism: Signs and Wonders Today*, (London: Hodder & Stoughton, 1985), 56-60.

15 *Fire from Heaven*, (London: Cassell, 1996), 306.

16 (London: DLT, 1992), 59.

17 (London: SCM Press, 1978), 379.

18 (Dublin: Dominican Publications, 1984) and *Values and Social Change in Ireland*, (Dublin: Gill & Macmillan, 1994) and McGreil, 'Religious Attitudes and Perceptions,' *Prejudice in Ireland Revisited* (Maynooth: St Patrick's College, 1996), 218-223.

19 Mon. Dec. 16th, 1996, 5.

20 'The Spirituality of the Future,' in *The Practice of Faith: A Handbook of Contemporary Spirituality*, (London: SCM Press, 1985), 21.

21 *Redemptoris Missio*, par. 42.

22 John Wimber, *Power Healing*, (London: Hodder & Stoughton, 1986), and *Power Evangelism*, (London: Hodder & Stoughton, 1985).

23 cf. Acts 5:12; 5:15; 6:8; 8:6; 8:13; 14:3; 15:12; 19:11; 28:9.

24 For more on this see Kelsey, *Healing*, 201ff.

25 *ST*, II-II Q. 178, A, 2.

26 *Pope Paul VI and The Spirit*, ed. Edward O Connor, (Notre Dame, Indiana: Ave Maria Press, 1978), 210-212.

APPENDIX

Some Patristic and Ecclesial Texts on the Charisms including the Charism of Faith

Some of the texts included here were either quoted in part, or adverted to, in the course of the book. Many of the translations are archaic and confusing. Where necessary I have made some changes in order to clarify the meaning of the texts.

1. The Shepherd of Hermas (c. 140-154 A.D.) *The Apostolic Fathers* trans., Glimm, Marique & Walsh, (New York: CIMA Publishing Co, 1947), 273-274. The ninth mandate, 'On Confidence in prayer':

> He said to me: 'Cast off indecision and doubt not in the least, when asking anything from God. Do not say "How can I ask and receive anything from the Lord after having committed so many sins?" Do not entertain such thoughts, but with your whole heart turn to the Lord and ask Him without wavering. You will learn his superabundant mercy. He will not leave you in the lurch. No! He will fulfil the request of your soul. God is not like human beings who bear a grudge. He is without malice and has mercy on what He has made. Cleanse your heart, then, of all the vanities of this world and of all the vices mentioned above. Then ask of the Lord and you will receive all. You cannot fail to obtain all your requests, provided you ask the Lord without wavering. However, if you waver in your heart, you will not receive a single one of your requests. Those who are divided in purpose are they who waver before the Lord and together fail to obtain any of their requests. But those who are wholly perfect in the faith ask everything with reliance on the Lord, and they receive, because they ask without wavering, without divided purpose. Every man of divided purpose will be

saved with difficulty, unless he repents. Cleanse your heart, then, of divided purpose, clothe yourself with faith, because it is strong, and put your trust in God, confident that you will receive every request you make of Him. Now, if some time or other, after having made it, you receive your request from the Lord rather slowly, do not doubt because you did not receive your soul's request quickly. In general you receive your request slowly because of some temptation or some shortcoming of which you are not aware. Do not let up, then, in the request of your soul. But, if in your request you grow faint and doubt, blame yourself and not the Giver. Be on your guard against this divided purpose, for it is evil and senseless. It uproots many from the faith, however strong in faith they are. For divided purpose is the daughter of the Devil and exceedingly wicked to the servants of God. Despise divided purpose and gain the mastery of it in everything by clothing yourself with strong and powerful faith. For faith promises all things and accomplishes them, but divided purpose, without confidence in itself, fails in all its works. You see, then, he said, 'that faith is from above, from the Lord, and its power is great, whereas divided purpose is an earthly spirit, from the Devil, lacking in power. Be subject, then, to the faith that has power and hold aloof from divided purpose that lacks power, and you will live to God as well as all who are of the same mind.'

2. St Ambrose of Milan, (387-388) 'Commentary on Psalm 118' in *The Faith of the Early Fathers* vol. 2, ed. William J. Jurgens, (Collegeville: The Liturgical Press, 1979), 165.

'Reward your servant' Ps 118:17 It is neither strange nor arrogant if David asks his Lord God for a reward for his heavy labors. It is the prerogative of faith and of justice to lay claim to the reward of God's favor. It is on this score that Peter is reproved; for when he was walking on the water his human feelings caused his doubt to be greater than the confidence inspired by his apostolic authority. In the gospel too we are taught to have faith and not to draw back from doing these things which are above a man ... It is not insolent arrogance but an innocent conscience which seeks a reward from Him whom you serve. Despair belongs to the crass sluggard; hope however, is an incentive to labor.

3. St Augustine, 'Sermon 80 on Mt 17:18-20' (410 A.D.) *Sermons: The Works of St Augustine, A Translation for the 21st Century* vol. 3, ed. John Rotelle, trans. Edmund Hill (Brooklyn, New York: New City Press, 1991), 354-355.

Let us pray, and put all our trust in God; let us live as he commands us, and when we stumble and stagger in this life, let us call upon him as the disciples called upon him, when they said, 'Lord increase our faith' Lk 17:5. Peter too was full of confidence, and staggered; yet he wasn't ignored and allowed to drown, but given a helping hand and set on his feet. Just what did he place his confidence in? It wasn't in himself, it was in the Lord. How's that? 'Lord if it is you, bid me to come to you over the water.' The Lord, you remember, was walking over the waters. 'If it is you, bid me to come to you over the water.' I know, you see, that if it is you, you have only to command, and it will happen. And he said, 'come.' He got out from his boat at his command, he began to tremble at his own weakness. And yet when he grew afraid he cried out to him: 'Lord, deliver me,' he said. Then the Lord took him by the hand and said, 'Man of little faith, why did you doubt?' Mt 14:28;30:31. It was he who invited him, he that delivered him when he tottered and staggered. This fulfilled what was said in the psalm, 'If I said, My foot has slipped, your mercy Lord, would come to my help' Ps 94:18.

So then there are two sorts of benefits, temporal ones and eternal ones. Temporal ones are such things as health, wealth, honor, friends, house, children, wife and the other things of this life through which we are travelling as foreigners. So let us place ourselves in the motel of this life, like travellers who are going to pass on, not like owners who are going to stay.

Eternal benefits, on the other hand, are first and foremost eternal life itself, the imperishibility and immortality of flesh and soul, the company of angels, the heavenly city, unfailing titles of nobility, a Father and a fatherland, the one beyond death, the other beyond enemies. We should be longing for these benefits with infinite desire, praying for them with tireless perseverance, not with long speeches, but with the evidence of our sighs. Desire is praying always, even if the tongue is silent. If you desire always, you are praying always. When does prayer nod off to sleep? When desire grows cold.

4. St Augustine, Sermon XXVI, 'Homilies on the Gospels,' *A Select Library of the Nicene and Post Nicene Fathers of the Christian Church* Vol. 6. ed. Philip Schaff, (Grand Rapids: Eerdmans), 341.

And Peter answered him, 'Lord if it is you, bid me to come to you on the water' Mt 14:28. For I cannot do this in myself, but in you. He acknowledged what he had in himself, and what he had from him, by whose will he believed that he could do that, which no human weakness was capable of doing. Therefore, 'if it is you, bid me to come;' because when you command, it will be done. What I cannot do by my unaided self, you can do by giving me the word of command. And the Lord said, 'Come' Mt 14:29. And without a shadow of doubt, at the behest of Him who called him, at the presence of Him who sustained him, at the presence of Him who guided him, without hesitation, Peter leaped down into the water, and began to walk. He was able to do what the Lord was doing, not in himself but in the Lord. 'For once you were darkness, but now you are light in the Lord' Eph 5:8. What no one can do in Paul, no one in Peter, no one in any other of the Apostles, this he can do in the Lord. Therefore Paul spoke well, when he said in a self deprecatory way that magnified the Lord, Was Paul crucified for you? Or were you baptised in the name of Paul? 1 Cor 1:13. So then, you are not *in* me, but together *with* me; not under me, but under Him.

Therefore Peter walked on the water by the bidding of the

Lord, knowing that he could not have this power of himself. By faith he had strength to do what human weakness could not do. These are the strong ones of the Church. Mark this, hear, understand, and act accordingly. For we must not deal with the strong on any other principle than this, in case they should become weak; but thus we must deal with the weak, that they may become strong. But the presuming on their own strength keeps many back from strength. No one will have strength from God, but he who feels himself weak of himself.

6. Eusebius *The History of the Church* 151, 'Rain sent from heaven in answer to Christian prayer' (It recalls what James says of the prayer of faith in Jm 5:18)

While Antoninus was still on the throne, it is on record that when his brother Marcus Aurelius Caesar deployed his forces for battle with the Germans and Samaritans, his men were parched with thirst and he was in a quandary. But the soldiers of the Melitene Legion, as it is called, through faith which has never wavered from that day to this, as they faced the enemy in their lines, knelt down on the ground, our normal attitude when praying, and turned to God in supplication. The enemy were astonished at the sight, but the record goes on to say that something more astonishing followed a moment later: a thunderbolt drove the enemy to flight and destruction, while rain fell on the army which had called on the Almighty, reviving it when the entire force was on the point of perishing from thirst ... Apolinarius ... says that from then on the legion which by its prayers brought about the miracle received from the emperor a title appropriate to the occurrence, being called in Latin the Thundering Legion.

7. Eusebius, *The History of the Church* 187, How Narcissus turned water to lamp oil as a result of the prayer of faith. (It recalls how Jesus turned water into wine in Jn 2:1-11)

Many stories of miracles wrought by Narcissus, handed down by generations of Christians, are told by members of the community. Among these they narrate the following tale of wonder. Once during the great all-night-long vigil of Easter, the deacons ran out of oil. The whole congregation was deeply distressed, so Narcissus told those responsible for the lights to draw water and bring it to him, and they obeyed him instantly. Then he said a prayer over the water, and instructed them to pour it into the lamps with absolute faith in the Lord. They again obeyed him, and, in defiance of natural law, by the miraculous power of God the substance of the liquid was physically changed from water into oil. All the years from that day to our own a large body of Christians there have preserved a little of it, as proof of that wonderful event.

8. *The Life of St Antony* xlviii, NPF 2nd series 4:209.

Martinian, a military officer, came and disturbed Antony. For he had a daughter afflicted by an evil spirit. But when he continued for a long while knocking at the door, and asking him to come out to pray to God for his child, Antony, not bearing to open, looked out from above and said, 'Sir, why do you call on me? I am a man like you. But if you believe in Christ whom I serve, go, and according as you believe, pray to God, and it will come to pass.' Straightway, therefore he departed, believing and calling on Christ, and he received his daughter cleansed from the devil.

9. St John Chrysostom, Homily LVII, 'Homilies on St Matthew,' *The Nicene and Post Nicene Fathers* vol X, ed. Philip Schaff, (Grand Rapids: Eerdmans, 1986), 355.

The disciples came to Jesus privately and said, 'Why could we not cast it out?' Mt 17:19. It seems to me that they were anxious and fearful, that they had lost the grace with which they had been entrusted. For they received power over unclean spirits (Mt 10:1). Taking him aside they asked him about the reason for their failure. They did so without shame (after all, they were only acknowledging in words what was already known); in a serious and private way. What did Christ reply? 'Because of your little faith. For truly, I say to you, if you have faith as a grain of mustard seed, you will say to this mountain, "Move from here to there," and it will move; and nothing will be impossible to you' Mt 17:20. Now if you say, 'When did they move a mountain?' I would reply, that in fact they did far greater things, having raised people from the dead. For it is one thing to move a mountain, it is quite another give life to a dead body. And some of the saints, who weren't as great as the apostles, are said to have actually moved mountains when there was a need for such action. The apostles would have done the same if it had been necessary. But there was no such need. So we can't fault them for not doing so. And besides, Jesus himself had not said, 'you *will* move mountains,' but rather, 'you will *be able* to move mountains.' So if they didn't do any mountain moving, it wasn't due to lack of ability. The had the ability to do even greater things. It is just that the need did not arise. In fact they may have moved a mountain, and the incident wasn't recorded, because we know that many of their miracles were not recalled in print. At this time however they were in a comparatively imperfect state. What was wrong? Why hadn't they the faith to act in power? The fact is, they weren't always the same. At one moment Peter was most blessed, and the next he is reproved by the Lord, as were the rest of the apostles for not understanding the parable of the leaven in Mt 16:6-12. And so it was at this time, the disciples were weak minded, as they often were before the crucifixion.

When Jesus speaks of faith here, he means the kind that works miracles. That is why he mentions the mustard seed of faith. He wants to convey its unspeakable power. For although the mustard seed is very small in size, it is unequaled in power. What Jesus is saying, is that even the smallest, but genuine amount of this kind of faith will be able to do great things. He went beyond the mustard seed, to mention the moving of mountains and concluded by saying that nothing would be impossible to the person of faith.

So you can marvel at the humility of the Apostles and the power of the Spirit. Their humility is a matter of facing that powerlessness and need. Instead of enabling them to grow by degrees to have the mustard seed of trust, it leads them to experience the rivers and mountains of faith springing up within them.

10. St John Chrysostom, homily 74, on Jn 14:8-15, in 'Homilies on St John' *The Fathers of the Church* vol. 41, trans. Sr. Thomas Aquinas Goggin, (New York: Fathers of the Church, Inc, 1960), 296-297.

Next, to show that not only could he do these works, but also others much greater than these, he continued in exalted terms. For he did not merely say: 'I can perform even greater works than these,' but something much more remarkable. He declared: 'I can even grant to others to perform still greater works than these. Amen, amen, I say to you, he who believes in me, the works that I do he shall also do, and greater than these shall he do, because I am going to the Father.' That is: 'In future the working of miracles is your prerogative because I am going away.' … To show that what he had said before was said with their weakness in mind. And the words, 'I am going to the Father,' have this meaning: 'I shall not disappear when I return to heaven, I will always remain with my followers.'

He said these things to encourage them. For it was probable that, because they did not understand the Resurrection, they would consider his words as sad news. Therefore, because of his all embracing care for them, he promised that they would perform for others the same good works that he performed. By this word of reassurance he was indicating that he would not only remain with them always, he would display even greater power through them.

11. The Charism in par. 12 of the *Dogmatic Constitution on the Church*, Catholic Desktop Library, Pauline Books and Media, 1994.

It is not only through the sacraments and the ministries of the Church that the Holy Spirit sanctifies and leads the people of God and enriches it with virtues, but, 'allotting his gifts to everyone according as He wills, He distributes special graces among the faithful of every rank. By these gifts He makes them fit and ready to undertake the various tasks and offices which contribute toward the renewal and building up of the Church, according to the words of the Apostle: "The manifestation of the Spirit is given to everyone for profit." These charisms, whether they be the more outstanding or the more simple and widely diffused, are to be received with thanksgiving and consolation for they are perfectly suited to and useful for the needs of the Church. Extraordinary gifts are not to be sought after, nor are the fruits of apostolic labor to be presumptuously expected from their use; but judgment as to their genuineness and proper use belongs to those who are appointed leaders in the Church, to whose special competence it belongs, not indeed to extinguish the Spirit, but to test all things and hold fast to that which is good.'

12. The charisms in par. 3 of the *Decree on the Apostolate of the Laity*, Catholic Desktop Library, Pauline Books and Media, 1994.

For the exercise of this apostolate, the Holy Spirit Who sanctifies the people of God through ministry and the sacraments gives the faithful special gifts also (cf. 1 Cor. 12:7), 'allotting them to everyone according as He wills' (1 Cor. 12:11) in order that individuals, administering grace to others just as they have received it, may also be 'good stewards of the manifold grace of God' (1 Peter 4:10), to build up the whole body in charity (cf. Eph. 4:16). From the acceptance of these charisms, including those which are more elementary, there arise for each believer the right and duty to use them in the Church and in the world for the good of men and the building up of the Church, in the freedom of the Holy Spirit who 'breathes where He wills' (John 3:8). This should be done by the laity in communion with their brothers in Christ, especially with their pastors who must make a judgment about the true nature and proper use of these gifts not to extinguish the Spirit but to test all things and hold for what is good (cf. 1 Thess 5:12, 19, 21).

13. The Charisms in par. 24 of *Decree on the role and Apostolate of the Laity*, Catholic Desktop Library, Pauline Books and Media, 1994.

> The Holy Spirit, while bestowing diverse ministries in Church communion, enriches it still further with particular gifts or promptings of grace, called charisms. These can take a great variety of forms both as a manifestation of the absolute freedom of the Spirit who abundantly supplies them, and as a response to the varied needs of the Church in history. The description and the classification given to these gifts in the New Testament are an indication of their rich variety. 'To each is given the manifestation of the Spirit for the common good. To one is given through the Spirit the utterance of wisdom, and to another the utterance of knowledge according to the same Spirit, to another faith by the same Spirit, to another gifts of healing by the one Spirit, to another the working of miracles, to another prophecy, to another the ability to distinguish between spirits, to another various kinds of tongues, to another the interpretation of tongues' (1 Cor 12:7-10; cf. 1 Cor 12:4-6, 28-31; Rom 12:6-8; 1 Pt 4: 10-1, 1).
>
> Whether they be exceptional and great or simple and ordinary, the charisms are graces of the Holy Spirit that have, directly or indirectly, a usefulness for the ecclesial community, ordered as they are to the building up of the Church, to the well-being of humanity and to the needs of the world. Even in our own times there is no lack of a fruitful manifestation of various charisms among the faithful, women and men. These charisms are given to individual persons and can even be shared by others in such ways as to continue in time a precious and effective heritage, serving as a source of a particular spiritual affinity among persons. In referring to the apostolate of the lay faithful the Second Vatican Council writes: 'For the exercise of the apostolate the Holy Spirit who sanctifies the People of God through the ministry and the sacraments gives the faithful special gifts as well (cf. 1 Cor 12:7), "allotting them to each one as he wills" (cf. 1 Cor 12:11), so that each might place "at the service of others the grace received" and become "good stewards of God's varied

grace" (1 Pt 4:10), and build up thereby the whole body in charity (cf. Eph 4:16).' By a logic which looks to the divine source of this giving, as the Council recalls, the gifts of the Spirit demand that those who have received them exercise them for the growth of the whole Church.

The charisms are received in gratitude both on the part of the one who receives them, and also on the part of the entire Church. They are in fact a singularly rich source of grace for the vitality of the apostolate and for the holiness of the whole Body of Christ, provided that they be gifts that come truly from the Spirit and are exercised in full conformity with the authentic promptings of the Spirit. In this sense the discernment of charisms is always necessary. Indeed, the Synod Fathers have stated: 'The action of the Holy Spirit, who breathes where he will, is not always easily recognised and received. We know that God acts in all Christians, and we are aware of the benefits which flow from charisms both for individuals and for the whole Christian community. Nevertheless, at the same time we are also aware of the power of sin and how it can disturb and confuse the life of the faithful and of the community.'

For this reason no charism dispenses a person from reference and submission to the Pastors of the Church. The Council clearly states: 'Judgment as to their [charisms'] genuineness and proper use belongs to those who preside over the Church, and to whose special competence it belongs, not indeed to extinguish the Spirit, but to test all things and hold fast to what is good (cf. 1 Thess 5:12 and 19-21),' so that all the charisms might work together, in their diversity and complementarity., for the common good.

Index